TOO DEEP
TO SHOVEL

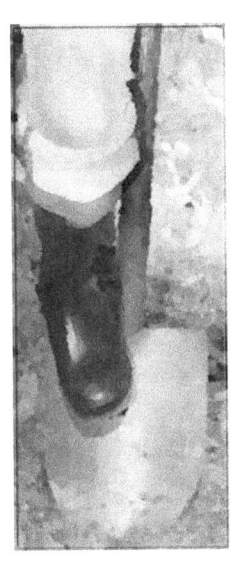

Too Deep to Shovel

ISBN # 144956867X
EAN-13 # 9781449568672
Revised Second Edition

If you have questions or comments concerning this book, please write:

The WORD Company USA
P. O. Box 878
Chewelah, WA 99109

TOO DEEP
TO SHOVEL

DIGGING INTO THE "MESSY ISSUES" FACING AMERICAN CITIZENS IN THE 21ST CENTURY

Foreword

Where I come from, old guys (and sometimes young guys) would sit around the coffee shop for hours and chat (the 20th Century chat room). When the stories got too outrageous and unbelievable, one of them would invariably say, "Gettin' deep, somebody get a shovel."

Looking, over the past few years, at where America is headed and how the American people are being "fed a line" a lot of the time, I am prepared to say, "Forget the barn boots! Get your chest waders; it's gettin' too deep to shovel!"

Time is of the essence if we are to save America from becoming something that most of us do not want it to be. It never ceases to amaze me how the vocal minority can carry so much weight in this country.

When you are up to your neck in "it," shoveling is <u>never</u> an effective solution. So with American 21st Century living examples like Mike Huckabee, Sarah Palin, Newt Gingrich, and Glenn Beck to inspire me, I'll just step up, speak out, and jump in with both feet to take a layman's look at what some of America's problems are and what some of the solutions could be.

G. S. Jones

TABLE OF CONTENTS

THE ECONOMY

Can You Say Mass Manipulation? • Carpooling Our Way to the Poorhouse • A Cure For What Ails Us • Stimulate This ... • 99 Models of Cars on the Line, 99 Models of Cars ... • The Sticky Issue of Employment – or Lack of It • Stealing From the Poor ... or the Middle Class ... or the Rich ... is Still Stealing! • Wars and Rumors of Wars • Why Do We Keep Rebuilding Where it Floods? Man Cannot Build a Dike God Cannot Put Water Over • Why are We Stimulating The Global Economy and Abandoning Our Own? • ☞ **REARVIEW MIRROR: WE CAN'T SAVE THE WHOLE WORLD, CAN WE? NO, WE CAN'T! NO, WE CAN'T! NO, WE CAN'T!**

POLITICS, GOVERNMENT AND TAXES

Running for a Reason • We Want it All; and Well, Yeah, Of Course We Want it NOW (or Yesterday)! • By the People and For the People, What a Concept! • An Extra-Large Dose of Reality • Where Did All the Good Ones Go? • Neighbors Representing Neighbors • Just Say "No" to Lobbyists and Career Politicians • Left and Right Usually Form a Working Pair • In Your House – In Your Business • A Runaway Train on a Bent Track • ☞ **REARVIEW MIRROR: TAXATION WITHOUT WHAT?**

OUR CHRISTIAN ROOTS

How Can We Forget Where We Began? •
Separation of Church and State: NOT! •
Insulation Without Isolation • Translate What?
• Patriotism: Living For God and Country •
REARVIEW MIRROR: ARE THE HOLES WE'RE
TEARING IN THE FABRIC TOO BIG TO MEND?

HEALTH AND HEALTH CARE

Health Care and Health Insurance are Not
Interchangeable Terms • Delineating the
"Fault Line" • Why Are We Killing Ourselves?
• Refine This ... Preserve That • Health in the
Garbage Can • Taking Care of #1 • Health
Care – Why Does it Cost SO Much? • The
"Plot" to Put Every American on at Least One
Pharmaceutical • Why Do We Cry "Foul" When
Oil Companies Post Record Profits, But Nobody
Seems to Notice that Pharmaceutical
Companies are Raking In Record Profits While
Feeding On People's Fears And Phobias? •
REARVIEW MIRROR: AN OPEN INVITATION

EDUCATION

Adding it Up • What's NOT Socialistic About
Today's Education Funding? • The Travesty of
Specialized Funds • Is Little Johnnie Ready for
Collage? (No, it's not a typo) • Budget Cuts
Due to Declining Enrollment • The Union
Factor • Reading, 'Riting, 'Rithmetic, 'Rections
... 'Rections!?! • TANSTAFL • How About We

Educate Our Own College Students First? •

DEDICATION

This book is dedicated to my incredibly wonderful husband and best friend, who is always willing to listen to my ramblings and supports me in all of my writing endeavors.

INTRODUCTION

Believe it or not, *Too Deep to Shovel* started out as a letter to the President. Once I realized my "letter" was going to be over 100 pages, I figured he would not read a letter that long – hence my thoughts became a book. He probably still won't read it, which is alright. My target audience at this point is the American people. You never know ...

The topics covered in this frank commentary are those I believe to be the most critical for Americans to find solutions to in the 21st Century.

It has been difficult to find a stopping point and "finish" the book, because it seems like something new comes up with every week that passes. I finally had to just quit writing, because I wanted it to be available prior to the November 2010 election. Now, here it is "twenty-'leven!"

I could go on and on ... but who would read it? Rather than write 500 pages, I have kept the book short so people will pick it up, wade through it, and then get busy and take action on some of these issues right away. We don't have any time to waste, friends and neighbors.

What you will read here, with the exception of a handful of noted references, are the opinions of an "average American citizen," which you are free to accept or reject. They are just opinions. There are bits and pieces of my "life" interspersed within these pages because it is within the act of living out our lives that we develop all of our opinions.

Are there any totally new ideas here? Probably not. But, I believe I am approaching these issues from some fresh angles that may prompt people to "get out of their easy chairs, pull their boots on, and pick up their shovels."

I have no illusions that everybody who reads *Too Deep to Shovel* will agree with everything I have to say. Even some of my close friends will not agree with everything I write in the pages that follow. Some people I know will be downright outraged, and a few might never speak to me again. *But there are some things that need to be said, and I may as well be the one to say them.*

Giving you a lot of answers is not my focus. I will ask some key questions that need asking, and my goal is for YOU to ask the hard questions of your governors, your school officials, your state and national legislators, your mayors and your insurance companies. And you might want to ask a few questions of the President, while you are at it!

Striking fear in your hearts is not my aim. I want to provoke you to action. I want you to get your "tall boots" out of the back of the closet, where you let them get buried by circumstance and apathy, and get ready to DO SOMETHING!

The time for, "Let somebody else handle it," is long past. Come on, America, let's dig ourselves out of our mess before "it" gets too deep to shovel!

"THE HEART OF THE WISE INCLINES TO THE RIGHT, BUT THE HEART OF A FOOL TO THE LEFT."

ECCL. 10:2

MESSY ISSUE #1

THE ECONOMY

**STIMULATE AMERICA'S WALLETS AND YOU WILL
STIMULATE THE AMERICAN ECONOMY**

[ma-nip-ū-lā´-shun]

The 1877 Webster definition of the word manipulation is, "a manual operation." That does not sound anything like what we consider to be the definition of the word manipulation as it is used in our American society today.

Mid-year in 2008, I began to feel very manipulated. And as the summer transitioned into fall, then into the fever pitch prior to the November election, it became more and more clear to me that someone, somewhere had a hand on what was happening with many areas of the American "economic downturn." Although I have my ideas, I never was able to pinpoint who was "pulling the strings." But it sure felt like <u>somebody</u> was.

The goal, as it appeared to me, was to make the majority of Americans SO desperate and dissatisfied that they would elect <u>anybody</u> to the President's office to get "change." Obviously, it was a brilliant strategy; and we will no doubt be paying for our ignorance and apathy for many years to come.

Commentators can say what they will about President Obama "inheriting" the financial situation that was out of control when he took his oath of office in January of 2009, but the events in the spring and summer of 2008, leading up to the election, may have been orchestrated completely beyond any control of the "fall-guy," President Bush.

Although many will disagree with me, the ultimate key, as far as I am concerned, was the price of oil, resulting in huge increases in the price of fuel for everything from airlines to oceanic shipping to trucking to the American automobile. The escalating price of oil, and consequently fuel, created a domino effect that worked its way into every area of our economy and our lives in a very short period of time.

In a matter of weeks, the cost of transporting everything (including themselves) sucked up money that people would have normally spent on other things. Businesses, from the grocery store to the tire store to the lumber yard and everything in between, had to almost immediately raise their prices because the cost of shipping their inventory nearly doubled virtually "overnight."

Restaurants, especially those that offered delivery of their food, suffered not only because the people eating their food had less money to spend on "eating out," but because the cost of purchasing and preparing the food and restaurant supplies had almost doubled.

The cost of transportation not only raised the cost on all consumer goods, but it also raised the cost on many services because "fuel surcharges" were added to many invoices for services all the way from the local plumber to the airlines. Even though fuel prices decreased dramatically by 2010 (compared to summer 2008), many companies continued to bill clients for fuel surcharges (no surprise to most of us).

People who had happily commuted an hour or more each way to work for years abruptly had to devote a far greater share of their budget to getting to and from work. Working folks, many of whom were already stretched to the max on their budgets, had to take money they would have spent on their mortgage or rent, utilities and groceries and put it into their gas tanks. Household, corporate, business – and even government – budgets began to implode and collapse.

Companies with large numbers of vehicles on the road as the core of their business suddenly had to lay off people to keep at least some of their vehicles in use. The same was true for public servants like police officers, paramedics and firefighters. Fuel is "life."

CARPOOLING OUR WAY TO THE POORHOUSE

Before long, the government was encouraging people to carpool, ride bicycles and motorcycles, and use public transportation to conserve fuel. People listened. People who were not already doing so began to carpool; and motorcycle sales, bicycle sales, and ridership on public transportation soared. People stayed close to home instead of taking long driving trips or flying vacations. Airline companies, still trying to recover from the devastation following Nine-Eleven, faltered once again due to both skyrocketing fuel costs and plunging ticket sales.

Guess what? Such a significant number of individuals and businesses cutting back on fuel purchasing and consumption caused the revenue from fuel taxes to drop rapidly and dramatically; and suddenly, all government entities that were funded by revenue from fuel taxes were in serious trouble! Saw that one coming! DUH! Where were the "experts" when they were thinking that strategy through?

With so much of their money going into fuel to get to the job they had to have to at least attempt to keep their heads above water, many people who were on the edge financially could not make their house (or rent) payments, even if they had never missed one in their lives. Some on-the-brink homeowners ultimately chose to stop making payments in hopes of a "home-mortgage bailout," which never came. Some just bailed out. Some became the victims of scammers passing themselves off as mortgage counselors.

When the number of home and investment/development property foreclosures escalated wildly, the banking institutions holding the mortgage notes suddenly discovered there was little or no money behind the "mortgage insurance" policies that had been attached to all of these loans that started out with 10% (or less) down so "the average Joe" could "live the American dream."

In addition, many of the individuals who had sold property on private notes to fund their retirement suddenly had, not only no income from the owner-financed property notes, but they now had court costs for foreclosure proceedings and then one or more houses or other investment properties they had to pay utilities and property taxes for and/or renovate so they might be marketable in a market where real estate was not selling.

Renters had to choose between feeding their children (and their gas tanks) and paying rent. When half (or more) of the tenants in an apartment complex cannot pay their rent, the property owner probably cannot pay his mortgage OR his taxes.

As things got worse and the international stock market began its plunge, people dependent on income from hard-earned investment accounts (many of which were heavily invested in "instruments" many of us had never heard of) suddenly had less and less income. If they had some money, people certainly were not going to spend it until they saw how things were going to go for the long term.

Income taxes not collected on income that is reduced, or completely ceases to exist, means a downturn in state and federal revenue and therefore cuts in government services available all the way down the line (even trickling into city and county budgets). Many of those budgets are locked into union contracts and cannot be altered easily, if at all.

People who still had jobs and who had a little money were hoarding it in case they got laid off or their hours or wages were reduced. Money not spent on goods and services translated immediately into less sales and excise tax revenue collected.

Many public schools are funded by local sales taxes but bound by union wage and benefit contracts.

School districts all across the country, some already on the verge of bankruptcy, were pushed to the limit, handing out pink slips by the thousands, in some cases.

Issues like DHL closing down their U.S. operation fueled the fire with large numbers of layoffs that devastated the local community. Just goes to show you that selling the company you have worked hard to build to a big foreign company is not always the best option. The "big guys" obviously did not consider the local community a priority. The original, local company that was bought out by the "big guys" cared about the local community – they WERE the local community.

What an incredible "house of cards," and I think one of the reasons we did not see it coming is because it was orchestrated – someone's gargantuan "experiment," with the American taxpayers as the guinea pigs.

A Cure For What Ails Us

Much of America's current economic suffering is the result of a dysfunction disorder that could be termed as "Unionafta Syndrome." This is a multi-symptom sickness that America has been suffering from, and foolishly not treating, for many years.

It still boggles my mind that those who push broad, open trade agreements do not seem to understand that every single thing we buy that is produced in another country is providing jobs and stimulating the economy in THEIR country, not ours! It does not seem like such a complicated concept to me. I am not sure why "they" don't get it.

I do understand that it is in the interest of selling our own goods and services that we enter into these agreements. Why we continue to allow the balance to be so skewed is a complete mystery to me, however. Eventually, we will not be manufacturing anything, so there will be no need to negotiate trade agreements – we will not have anything to "trade."

The ONLY cure for what ails us in America is to keep as many jobs as possible at home. Right now, we are far too dependent on other countries, not only to provide things we want, but for things we need.

I am sure we "make" things in America today, but it seems to me like we do not make enough. When our well pump guy pulled our pump and worked on it, he indicated that it was not possible to purchase a water-well pump made in America. I have not researched that yet; but if it is true, it certainly looks like a niche for a manufacturing business to me. Americans should have at least a choice in purchasing an item that is made in America over an item that is made somewhere else in the world.

Maybe we could go back to having people, instead of machinery and robots, make things in the factories we DO have. Now there is a novel idea. Look how many people that would put back to work!

American unions played an important role when they were created. But, I saw as many as 25 years ago, that our economy could not continue to thrive with mandatory wage and benefit increases working their way into so many areas of both business and government. Made in America, all too often, is equivalent to "I cannot afford it." Can the average American afford to purchase the average "American-made" product in the 21st Century?

This is not news to anybody; but maybe some folks need a reminder: *When the cost of labor goes up, the cost of everything labor touches goes up. So the cost of "living" goes up.* So the labor unions demand a cost-of-living raise. Then the cost of labor that produces or transports anything goes up. So the cost of everything labor touches goes up. Consequently, the cost of "living" goes up – again. So the labor unions demand a cost-of-living raise ... I think you get my point.

So why don't we GET IT? Why do we keep riding this circular train to nowhere?

STIMULATE THIS ...

[*stim ' ū-lus*]

Do you think it is possible somebody is playing a horrible joke on us and has changed the word to [*stim ' ū-LESS*]?

What makes my blood boil? How about the story on the news in early 2010 about the "stimulus money" that is providing 3,000 manufacturing jobs overseas to create parts for wind turbine towers so we can create 300 jobs in Texas.

Are we NUTS?!? With our access to "information" today, how can this have slipped past the citizenry? Why are we not manufacturing engines and parts for wind generators in America? Do we need a factory? Then take some of the stimulus money and build one. It cannot cost the American people any more in the long term than giving another country 3,000 jobs for THEIR people while our people struggle to make ends meet or face losing everything they have worked for.

Why aren't our legislators who are doling out these funds embarassed to be called "servants of the American people"? They should be too embarassed to even come out in public, much less run for re-election! Why can't they see what is right and JUST DO IT?

Why are we willing to settle for creating 300 jobs when we could be creating 3,000? How are we ever going to recover economically with this minimal level of job creation and this kind of "reasoning"?

With interest, my family watched God's economic stimulus plan played out "Back East" in February of 2010. He directly stimulated tens of thousands of people to pay someone to dig them out of the snow. I never did hear a dollar figure on that one, but it was probably more beneficial in putting real dollars in real people's pockets than much of the "stimulus" money has so far. My family has personally experienced similar short-term "natural" economic stimulus "packages," with record snowfalls in Alaska

13

in the winter of 1989-90 and in our own eastern Washington snow country several times in the last two decades.

When congress was working on the stimulus bill, some of us had a simple solution to stimulating the economy. If the President and congress had put the total dollar amount of the "stimulus" bill directly in the hands of the American people, we would have been almost immediately overwhelmed by the economic recovery it would have created.

First, people would have had to deposit the million or more dollars they received in one or more bank accounts. That would most definitely have helped the banks' "bottom lines."

Second, people would have made purchases of items all the way from groceries to new carpet and furniture for their homes to cars, trucks, boats and motor homes with their new-found "wealth."

People would have stayed in their homes or purchased new ones, stocked their pantries, spiffed up their wardrobes, and stimulated American businesses all the way from the corner quick stop to Microsoft.

Business owners (or wanta-be business owners) would have expanded (or started) businesses of all sizes that would employ hundreds of thousands of people in a broad range of career areas.

Beyond the private sector, virtually everything that is bought or sold generates tax revenues for the government, all the way from the local community to the U. S. government. Outside of the fact that "big government" is way too big and needs paring down, how could collecting additional tax revenue so that cities, counties, states, and school districts can meet their budgets have a downside? There would have been a huge increase in income taxes, sales and excise taxes, and property taxes collected as a result of such a "stimulus."

I do not believe it is too late to undertake a stimulus of this sort. Now, don't get me wrong, I do NOT believe that the government should be handing out money. But, if they are going to hand it out with us not even knowing where it is going or whether it will actually benefit anybody (and our grandchildren are going to have to pay for it), putting it in our hands is the way it could have the most benefit for the most American people.

Put the stimulus money directly in the bank accounts of all American citizens and the economy will recover in record time.

It is probably unrealistic to think that making "rich folks" out of every American citizen is a good plan for the long term. But, I believe it deserves more merit than what is currently being "done."

You say such a stimulus plan would have created a "false economy"? Who says we don't have a false economy now? If it looks like duck ...

The question is not: What could the American people have done? The question is: What COULDN'T the American people have done with this stimulus money in their pockets and their bank accounts?

A couple of decades ago, watching an advertisment for a car company that was proudly offering 99 different models, I could not fathom how anybody could possibly need that many choices. Common sense tells me that manufacturing that many "models" <u>has</u> to make them ALL cost more in the long run.

People who need a pickup truck will buy one even if there are only three "models" available. If they need a pickup and do not have any other choices, they are going to buy one of the three. They NEED the truck. If they just "want" a pickup, they might have to just get over it and choose from what is available.

Nobody needs 99 models of cars from one company. And that does not count the, perhaps, 99 models from each of the other car companies, in addition to the first 99. Do you know how many car models that is? Do you know how ridiculous that really sounds when you think about it?

My husband uses the term "affluenza" frequently. It is such a problem in America that PBS aired more than one documentary program about it in the 1990s; and a number of books have been written on the subject. I have to agree that it is one of the critical problems in our country. It has to do with far more than 99 models of cars from one company, but the cars are one example of an increasing addiction there does not seem to be any cure for.

We seem to never be satisfied, satiated. We always want more – more food, more clothing, a bigger and better car, a bigger and better house, more stuff. Well, people, you are getting up to your neck in your stuff and you need to get the shovel out before "it" buries you and you suffocate!

THE STICKY ISSUE OF EMPLOYMENT – OR LACK OF IT

Let's see – I am in fairly good financial shape and my wife is still working. They are going to extend my unemployment benefits another 12 weeks. How hard am I going to look for a job? Maybe not that hard. Why should I?

And then you throw the term "seasonally-adjusted" into the data. Wake up, people, there is ALWAYS an off-season, with a country as varied as ours is from coast to coast and North to South. The unemployment rate is ALWAYS seasonally adjusted somewhere in America – especially in summer!

I keep hearing the term "under-employed," and it is being said that the unemployment count should include the number of people who have been unemployed so long they have quit looking. Sounds like a less-than-creative way to manipulate numbers to me.

17

The extended, extended, extended unemployment benefits have to run out eventually; and when they do, we are going to get a much more realistic picture of what the American economy really looks like. And it will become abundantly clear that the current "stimulus" is just a smokescreen to get the Democrats through to the November 2010 elections.

The only cases I know of people who have quit looking for work are:

1) those who have made a decision, based on their financial situation, to have one spouse stay at home because they can afford to do so,

2) those who have decided to further their education and have gone back to college (there are a lot of those; their college debt will catch up to them soon enough and that will create a whole new problem nationwide),

3) those who have opened their own business or consulting firm,

4) those who can no longer draw unemployment and are no longer being "tracked" by anybody in their job search (some of whom may be working – under the table – and are not actually "unemployed" at all).

My family has personal acquaintances who have spent considerable time "under-employed" in recent years because they are financially able to take less money than they were making prior to a serious job loss. It does not mean they are dissatisfied, or that they are suffering financially. It just means that they are willing and able to live on less income than they had in their previous job and can wait as long as necessary for their next "dream job" opportunity.

Obviously, there are people who have to make sacrifices to live on less income. And most of those people are probably dissatisfied – perhaps even "suffering," to a certain extent. We do not live in a perfect world. Too many of us are living too close to the edge of financial disaster. Many people are forced to scale back spending in tough economic times – shopping more carefully, re-prioritizing their needs and wants, and ultimately becoming <u>content</u> with less income and less "things." My famiy is one of those scaled-back families.

To date, I have not ever personally drawn unemployment. Frankly, I never felt I could "afford" to wait until it kicked in. In the decade when I was single, anytime I was without a "permanent" job, I worked for a "temp" agency and was always able to meet my monthly obligations until something "permanent" or "better" came along. One of those temp placements ultimately led to a permanent job.

Oh, I know – "way back when" things were different than they are today. If you look around and really SEE things as they are, they are not that much different, however. Our expectations are different. Our "wants" are different. The "house of cards" many people built for themselves only needed one little breeze to crumble and tumble it into a pile of rubble. The financial nightmare that occurred in 2008 was a tornado, not a breeze, regardless of whether or not it was purposefully created.

During my high school years, I spent my summers working in various local farming occupations (tying hops, driving tractor for a hay crew, topping corn, etc.) In the early 1970s, among my other field work opportunities, I picked apples for a small, local orchard.

On a bright, sunny morning in the shade of the apple trees, I had a conversation with a man who told me that he was out to prove to his family that there were plenty of jobs available. As this probably-thirty-something Caucasian man told it, some of his siblings had been complaining that they could not find jobs. His "lesson" to them was to go get a new job every day for a year. And he was halfway through his year when he arrived at the apple orchard where I met him. He had literally sought and attained a different job every day for half a year. Although I never knew if he made it through the entire year, my guess would be that he did. Maybe he will read this, recognize himself, and drop me a note.

None of the situations mentioned in this sub-chapter are an indication of a national financial condition. Our own personal family income is roughly 1/3 of what it was 15 years ago, but we have made carefully-thought-out choices to get to this point and are not suffering in any way (at least until "health care reform" hits us in the pocketbook in due time).

Frankly, my husband and I are able to get by nicely without making enough money to even wave at what appears to be the <u>low</u> end of "middle income." We are "comfortable" and we do not do without anything we truly need. I heard they were going to subsidize health care plans for families with income up to $75,000 per year. If our combined income was $75,000 per year, we would not need a subsidy, we could afford the most expensive health insurance plan offered by any company today.

We don't have to "keep up with the Joneses" – we ARE the Joneses – and keeping up with us is not as difficult as most people believe!

STEALING FROM THE POOR ... OR THE MIDDLE CLASS ... OR THE RICH ... IS STILL STEALING!

In the story, Robin Hood stole from the rich. His motives may have been noble, but it was still stealing. In America, in so many ways, we are stealing from the poor ... and the middle class ... and the rich. Friends and neighbors, stealing is stealing!

I am opposed to our nation spending one dime on space travel, foreign aid, or any kind of "non-essential expense" until every individual in America that wants a job has one, and until every American family is secure in having the roof of their choice over their heads. We need to shore up Social Security and Medicaid for the truly needy in our country and get everybody else out of both programs.

Decades after initial stories were released about astronomical government waste, there does not seem to be ANY change. I could scarcely believe my ears when I heard the dollar figure just for the SIGNS telling passersby that their tax dollars are funding the "stimulus-funded" road and bridge projects currently underway across the country. Great stimulus for the sign company. Good thinking ... you bet ... Who got the contract for the signs?

I would like to challenge any and all of our senators and representatives to come here and live our lives for a few months. Surely they do not all come from wealthy backgrounds. At least some of them had to have come from modest means, or maybe even abject poverty, and can truly grasp what the American "middle class" is going through in this economy. How do they fail to understand?

Our household has gone from $100,000+ per year to $70,000 per year, to well under $50,000 per year for two working adults. We have six grown children, one of them married and three of them in college.

We live in a comfortable, custom-designed home that has energy-efficient appliances and windows. We do not own an air conditioner (and do not want one because they consume too much electricity), even though it gets up to 100° occasionally in the summer where we live. We have two automobiles, one is eight years old and one is seven years old. Both are in great condition, with low mileage on both of them.

We can survive financially because we budget carefully and stick to our budget. We only get to take a "real" vacation trip every five years or so, but we travel to a nearby state to visit relatives at least twice each year. Nothing about our lives is extravagant. But, on the other hand, nothing about our lives is inadequate, either.

My husband goes to the doctor every two years for a physical because it is required for his job. He has an occasional cold. I go to the doctor every few years for a "female checkup" and have an occasional cold or 24-hour flu bug. We are educated and intelligent and perfectly capable of finding out how to treat most common ailments and minor injuries. Our children are also educated and intelligent and perfectly capable of finding out how to treat most common ailments and minor injuries. It is how we were raised and how we raised our children.

We can currently afford a catastrophic insurance plan for both of us. But if the price doubles with "health care reform," then we are faced with the choice of selling one of our vehicles or making some other sacrifice. We are healthy, hard-working American patriots. Why should we be forced to buy insurance we cannot afford or face being fined for our failure to comply? It makes me sick to my stomach to think that our freedom-loving nation has come to the point where such a thing is even suggested!

Who wants to live in a country that will put you in jail if you do not buy a health insurance policy? The government is taking money from all of us to blatantly and inexplicably squander and waste day after day, month after month, year after year. When are we going to stand up and take responsibility as "we the people"? We are being robbed folks, fleeced, bilked out of thousands and sometimes tens of thousands of our hard-earned dollars by a government too big to watchdog itself. How many more years are we going to allow the people who represent US to throw away our money? Maybe you can afford to throw money out the window, but I cannot!

WARS AND RUMORS OF WARS

Unfortunately, one of the major reasons our national deficit has grown so large in recent years is the extremely high cost of carrying on military action in several areas across the sea. I do not even WANT to know how much this is costing – and how much money is being totally wasted on contracts for services to our military overseas that are billing (or is that bilking) the U. S. taxpayers for hundreds and hundreds of millions of dollars. For what purpose? We will be fighting the Taliban and Al-Qaeda forever, most likely. *It is their lifetime passion and pursuit.*

Supporting our soldiers is something I have always done. I never thought I would say it, but we need to bring all of our soldiers home and get ready for a fight here! I am more convinced than ever that we will be attacked from WITHIN in the near future.

And send Iraq a bill for services rendered and encourage them to compensate us for what we have done already. Aren't there oil wells in Iraq that are making money? Can they not participate financially in the new "lease on life" we have provided?

There is no doubt that every American life that is lost in pursuit and preservation of freedom in Afghanistan, Iraq and elsewhere in the world in combat is tragic and devastating. However, when you look at the statistics on people who die on American soil every day from causes all the way from intentional gunshots to heart disease, the numbers take on a somewhat different meaning.

Not everyone may share my opinion, but the family of a fallen soldier is not hurting more than the family of a co-worker of mine who died suddenly from a massive heart attack at age 50, or the local family who lost all six of their children in a single auto accident.

Is it true that over 10,000 people every year die from intentional gunshot wounds in the U.S.? Over 40,000 from motor vehicle accidents? From all causes, more than two million people die in America annually? We will probably always be helping someone, somewhere with our military, but we need to consider the idea that we may actually have bigger "battles to fight" at home right now.

America, as a whole, has not been fully in agreement on fighting a "war" since the second world war. Although I understand the reasoning behind what we are doing in Iraq and Afghanistan, I am not certain we should be there now; and I am 100% sure that our National Guard should never have been sent overseas. We need our National Guard at HOME!

If nothing else, we could man the Mexican border with so many National Guard soldiers that nobody could get across it. Let's do this, America!

So much of the problem, both in Afghanistan and in Mexico has to do with huge drug cartels fighting for control (and money). Why is there so much demand for their "product"? What can we do to change that permanently? People, we must get a handle on the drug war that is spilling over our southern border and costing us billions of dollars as a society; and we must do it now!

Bring home our National Guard and let them serve their country and protect freedom here. Even if the "bill" continues to be high to pay and provision our soldiers, they will at least be on our home soil making a real difference in American people's lives.

We are being invaded. If you do not agree, then watch and read the news for a couple of weeks. Arizona is trying to defend not only their land, but their people and their economy. Park the entire National Guard of every non-border state and a few thousand soldiers from each of our military branches on the borders of Arizona, New Mexico, Texas and California for just two weeks and see what happens. Then leave the majority of them there for six months and perhaps we will be done with it!

The savings to the U. S. taxpayers will be huge!

WHY DO WE KEEP REBUILDING WHERE IT FLOODS? MAN CANNOT BUILD A DIKE GOD CANNOT PUT WATER OVER

Dozens of years ago, when I first heard about people getting flooded out <u>again</u> on the big rivers in the other half of the country, I wondered, at the time, why anybody allowed people to rebuild where they had lost everything. It was my opinion that, if they desired to rebuild there, they should not be allowed to have insurance cover future losses – and therefore an insurance company (and everyone who pays premiums to that company) would not get stuck with the bill on <u>another</u> loss at the same potentially-soggy location. I am still looking for an answer to that question, even as we watch news reports of more flooding in several areas of the country.

There seems to be a never-ending stream of natural disaster related reconstruction projects across the country every year – between wildfires, floods, tornadoes, and hurricanes. Some of the reconstruction is being paid for by insurance companies; some by the government (including FEMA); and some by folks who believe in taking care of themselves (perhaps with the help of their local community). But it is a huge amount of money!

No matter how much insurance companies charge all of their customers, I do not see how they can continue to pay out billions of dollars in coverage for losses in storms and floods and fires (especially as the prices of the homes get higher and higher, sometimes into the millions of dollars) over and over and over again – regardless of whether the insurance is through a private company or the U.S. Government.

It does not make economic sense at all to me to let people rebuild where losses have occurred multiple times. If they insist on rebuilding in such a location, they should be prevented from purchasing an insurance policy and be "on their own." I am not an economist, but I am not an idiot either. Paying to rebuild the same houses and other buildings over and over again in the same location is indirectly costing me money, and I cannot afford it! Can you?

Obviously, natural disasters have sucked up astronomical amounts of insurance company profits, especially in the past 20 years. Spring 2010 was no different – record snowfalls, rising rivers – and summer 2010 is not looking much better.

By the way, how much petroleum is used to make all of those sand bags and where do they go afterward? Do they end up in the ocean when they do not hold back floodwaters? Are they emptied and recycled? Spend days building sandbag dikes 10' high so 16' of water can go over them anyway. Great economic stimulus for the company that makes the bags.

There are some "smart communities" that have chosen to relocate and rebuild the entire town on higher ground where the possibility of future flooding is remote. But those are few and far between. Strategies such as this should be the norm, not the exception. Flood "management" is obviously not working particularly well.

We cannot control fires or floods, hurricanes or tornadoes. Wildfires are just as likely to be started by lightning as they are by humans. Why aren't we working harder to protect ourselves with our structures and our landscaping? Or are we? If it is happening on a broad scale, I am not hearing about it in the news!

Let's direct some stimulus money toward designing tornado- and hurricane-proof houses and fireproof landscaping. Move some towns or neighborhoods away from flood zones permanently. Quit stacking houses on unstable, potentially dangerous terraces up the sides of foothills and cliffs. Follow up and make sure the stimulus "investment" in new construction and landscaping technology gets implemented in areas that are prone to fires and floods, hurricanes and tornadoes.

My family lives in the mountains on the side of a forested hill. We developed landscaping that prevents a fire from running right up next to our siding, which is cement and will not burn. A couple of sprinklers on the roof and we are pretty well protected from wildfire loss, even though we are in the middle of wildfire country on a mountain that has seen fire before.

Is there something keeping us from being sensible and reasonable in our materials and landscaping designs? If so, then what is it going to take to change our way of thinking?

WHY ARE WE STIMULATING THE GLOBAL ECONOMY AND ABANDONING OUR OWN?

Yes, we have to support the economies of other nations to a certain extent, *but certainly not to the utter ruination of our own*! At some point, we have to say "enough" and stop helping others until we are finished helping ourselves. We need every dime at home today. If you do not believe that, you are deceiving yourself. Every time I hear it stated that we are going to send tens and sometimes hundreds of millions of dollars in "aid" to another country, I cringe. We do not have any money to send anyone. We have a DEFICIT!

Of course, we feel compassion for those who need "rescuing" in other countries. But, I feel sorry for my neighbors, too. Some of them lost their homes almost 10 years ago when a local aluminum plant shut down because they could not compete with foreign companies.

When this plant shut down in response to global competition, many families had to move away from our area because there were no jobs here to replace the 300 that were lost in a community of under 2,500 population. Home foreclosures skyrocketed. Families were torn out by the roots and transplanted elsewhere – wherever they could find work.

This is real life, people. Nobody "bailed" the folks in our little community out. How do you think people who lost their homes here feel when they see the government bending over backward to help out those losing their homes today? There is nothing fair or equitable about that! Why help one and not the other? It was the "economy" that was the primary factor both then and now. How about a retro bailout for those who have "been there, done that"?

How about all of the people in Alaska who lost their homes in the late 1980s because of huge layoffs in the oil industry? Can those thousands of people get a retro bailout? "The economy" caused the problem, but nobody helped them. In fact, so many people in Alaska were out of work and losing their homes that the mortgage companies created new rules at that time so they could go after people's motor homes and boats and other assets because the houses they were foreclosing on had negative equity in a market where nothing was selling. Sound familiar? What is different about today? *Government intervention ... that's what!*

My own family had negative equity in our home in Alaska for more than 10 years, but we stuck it out until the market recovered, with no help from the government – and no OFFER of help.

American people, American businesses, our economy should come first and EVERYBODY ELSE should come after that. Period.

I remember watching a news report about China's preparation for the Olympics and how they had to shut down many of their manufacturing facilities to literally clear the air in their nation so athletes from all over the world could breathe reasonably clean air while they were competing.

During this broadcast program, it was made clear that China did not discontinue all of their manufacturing – they took many of their facilities to other nations and continued producing goods. Just because a tag does not say "Made in China," does not mean the dollars spent on that product are not ultimately supporting the economy of China.

How many products has China purchased from the United States this year? They may practically "own" us, but are they purchasing products manufactured in the United States? How many billions of dollars have we pumped into THEIR failing economy? Into other failing international economies?

Even American auto companies only "assemble" vehicles in many of their plants here. How many of the parts "automakers" assemble are made in the U.S.? How many of them are made in another country? How many cars are actually "built" in America? Any?

I do not see how we can continue to operate these backward trade agreements with other nations and keep our own country economically afloat. This is genuinely an area where it will soon become too deep to shovel our way out of the pit we are sinking into.

By the way, are the hundreds of thousands of plastic bags, floating booms, and "hazmat" suits being used in the effort to clean up BP oil on the beaches on the U. S. gulf coast made in China? I hope not! What a slap in the face to out-of-work Americans that would be!

WE CAN'T SAVE THE WHOLE WORLD, CAN WE? NO, WE CAN'T! NO, WE CAN'T! NO, WE CAN'T!

America's citizens and taxpayers are stimulating economies all over the planet. Sometimes, it seems like we are stimulating everybody's economy but our own. This cannot continue without dire consequences for all of us.

Our national (and global) economy is so much different than it was even 20 years ago. Let's face it, friends and neighbors, America cannot save the world, although we should do as much as we are able to without harming our own country and citizens.

Humanitarian aide is wonderful, if we have money to spare. Do we, as a country, have money to spare today? Looking at the display showing the national debt skyrocketing every day, I think not. Are we going to pump hundreds of millions we do not have into helping Russia and Pakistan, now? Do we have enough ink and paper for our currency printing machinery to do that?

Why <u>are</u> we sending so much money to other countries when so many of our own people need our support? I heard that more than 90% of Haiti is still in the state it was in following the earthquake. After all of the billions of dollars pumped into Haiti, both before and after the devastating quake, how can that be true? We, as a country, did not have hundreds of millions of dollars we could "spare" to send to Haiti. So why did we even offer to send it?

We have tens of thousands of people flooded out, burned out, and windblown out of their homes and businesses in <u>America</u>. *There comes a point when we have to make the hard choice and take care of our own FIRST.*

LOOKING TO THE FUTURE

- DO WHATEVER IT TAKES TO PUT MORE MONEY INTO THE POCKETS OF THE AMERICAN PEOPLE AND WE WILL BE MAKING HISTORY WITH THE ECONOMIC RECOVERY THAT OCCURS AS A RESULT.

- JOBS WILL BE CREATED WHEN PEOPLE HAVE MORE MONEY IN THEIR POCKETS TO SPEND THAN THEY NEED AND ARE NOT AFRAID TO LET GO OF IT!

- THE IDEA OF LENDING STIMULUS MONEY TO SMALL BUSINESSES ACROSS OUR COUNTRY IS COMMENDABLE, AND ADVISABLE; HOWEVER, IT IS NOT GOING TO CREATE

THE SHEER NUMBERS OF WELL-PAYING JOBS IT WILL TAKE TO RESTORE OUR ECONOMY.

- HOW ABOUT WE START WITH PRODUCING OUR OWN OIL AND OTHER FORMS OF ENERGY — AND MANUFACTURING OUR OWN GOODS!

- IF WE ARE GOING TO SPEND IT ANYWAY, TAKE THAT STIMULUS MONEY AND REPAIR EVERY FAULTY BRIDGE AND CRUMMY ROAD IN THE NATION INSTEAD OF STUDYING WHY PIGS STINK! I DID SEE SOME EVIDENCE OF BRIDGEWORK IN OUR PART OF THE COUNTRY FUNDED BY "ARRA" IN THE SUMMER OF 2010. THEY ARE STILL ONLY TEMPORARY JOBS, HOWEVER. ROADS AND BRIDGES ARE NOT PERMANENT JOBS THAT KEEP A MAN AT HOME WHERE HE CAN TAKE CARE OF HIS WIFE AND RAISE HIS CHILDREN.

- CASH FOR CLUNKERS AND OTHER ASPECTS OF THE OBAMA "STIMULUS PACKAGE" HAVE BEEN DEBATED AND DEBATED, SO I AM NOT GOING TO DELVE INTO THAT NONSENSICAL NIGHTMARE. WE NEED TO LEARN OUR LESSONS AND MOVE FORWARD, HOPEFULLY WITH REAL STIMULUS FOR THE AMERICAN ECONOMY IN THE NEXT FEW YEARS.

MESSY ISSUE #2

POLITICS, GOVERNMENT AND TAXES

OBIT ...

"HERE LIES THE CITIZEN LEGISLATOR, CUT
DOWN IN HIS PRIME BY GREED AND
CORRUPTION. WHAT A TRAGIC LOSS TO OUR
COMMUNITY AND OUR STATE."

If you are running for office in the next decade in America, there are things you need to consider:

You had better be a moral man or woman we can trust implicity with our lives, our children's lives, and our grandchildren's lives and who will not be in the news next week for flying off to somewhere to visit your lover while your wife and children sit at home blindly believing you are out diligently serving your constituents.

Your sole purpose in serving as a citizen legislator had better be to improve the lives of everyone in your constituency, not just the ones with fat wallets!

If your constituents are just a stepping stone to higher office for you, please do us all a favor and do not file the paperwork to run at all. *This does not mean you should not aspire to a higher office, you just need to make sure you do a good job for those who elected you, every step of the way on your journey upward.*

Your platform had better be centered around JOBS – large numbers of permanent, well-paying, useful, private-sector jobs. Jobs where a man can buy a house for his family and stay in his community for a lifetime. Jobs where a family can start their kids and graduate them in the same school district. Jobs that help make America energy independent (including developing non-renewable resources when we genuinely need to).

Jobs that drive the American economy back to prosperity and financial security, not five or ten years down the road, but NOW.

Whether you are running for State or National office, you must support making America the best it can be before we spend even one dime on "foreign aid" or to send anybody to the moon and stars.

WE WANT IT ALL, AND, WELL YEAH, OF COURSE WE WANT IT NOW (OR YESTERDAY)!

Who do you know that does NOT want the highways to be smooth, the stoplights to be working (complete with multiple turn lane signals), and a new freeway to make it faster to get from one side of the city to the other?

We want sewer and water and electricity available (and working 24/7/365) everywhere. We want the police in two minutes or less and a free ambulance in four. We want a fire truck immediately, no matter the time or place.

We want affordable natural gas, high-speed Internet, and cable TV at our door, no matter where we live. And a five-bar cell phone signal on every "inch" of the U. S. map, no matter which service provider we are with.

We want our schools to have the latest textbooks, a SmartBoard™ in every classroom, a computer lab in every other classroom, high-tech this and top-of-the-line that. Tax dollars wane, union contracts incrementally increase, enrollment declines, nobody wants to "sacrifice" their department or program. We want every child to graduate with a high "employability" rating and ready to attend college if he or she chooses to do so (and can afford to).

School heating bills rise in cold country and air conditioning bills rise in hot country. Fuel costs increase for buses running longer and longer routes. Buses cost more and more as they get smarter transmissions and automatic snow chains, while the children still sit on a board with some foam and smelly, potentially-toxic petroleum-based vinyl stapled to it.

The problem is, too many of us want "someone else" to pay for it. After all, who can afford all of that? We can't. Someone else is always the American taxpayers. There is not anybody else!

Obviously, a mix of state and federal dollars are involved in roads and utilities. If you do not think taxpayer dollars are involved in the cost of the phone line that comes across your lawn, you have not been paying attention (especially in rural areas) to utility subsidies. The American taxpayers are reportedly even subsidizing cell phones for some "low-income" folks in this country. Why?

Anyone who has played the computer games that simulate city building found out very quicky that when you build "suburbs" on the edges of your city, your suburban residents want full utilities right away; and before long they also want a police station, a hospital, and a fire station nearby – not 10 miles away where you put the original services in your initial city plan. Real life is not that much different. Who do you think developed the video games?

During long, cold winters in snow country, we want all of the roads plowed and sanded before we drive to work in the morning. We want the power back on in minutes, not days, when a transmission line goes down in an ice storm. We are spoiled rotten, and we know it.

What a blessing that "somebody else" is paying for it! Wake up, people, WE are "somebody else"! No matter the source, ultimately we all pay for it.

You say you already knew that? Well, then how do you expect to achieve a significant decrease in the amount of taxes you pay? Do you need your long-handled shovel for this one? Do you need someone to show you which end of the shovel goes in the ground?

If we were to make a list of the services and benefits we are willing to give up to save taxpayer money, yours would probably be pretty short, like mine.

Some cities are turning off every other streetlight to save electricity. That is probably okay with you unless your bus stop or your favorite parking spot is under the one that is turned off.

Some city, county and state governments are closing their offices one day a week. That is probably alright, unless you are the nearby daycare provider who just lost 20% of her income because her clients are now home with their children one more day a week.

Here is a little assignment for you. Make a list of 10 people in your circle of friends and acquaintances who you think would be willing to give up ANYTHING they have now to save taxpayer dollars. Can't think of 10? How about 2? How about one? How about you? Are YOU willing to give up anything to save tax dollars?

Of course, there are areas (vast quantities of them) where government agencies and entities could – and SHOULD – cut spending. We need to be diligently working on that. I am almost sure I remember candidate Obama saying he was going to do that. He has probably just been too busy with other things to get to it. *Maybe he is figuring on tackling that task in his second term as President ...*

My theory is that government is feeding and flourishing on a virus called "vastus governmentitis." Is there a pill for that? Can we recommend "debt counseling" for the government? How about if we insist on it!

Call the President's financial "czar" and give him the phone number for the debt reduction hotline! That is what they would recommend for you if you blew out your budget like they have been!

Better yet, call the President and ask him when he is going to go through that budget line by line and eliminate all the "waste."

By the People and For the People, What a Concept!

With complete disbelief, I listened to news reports of our elected senators and representatives who hoped to push through the beginnings of the new health care bill before they returned home for their Christmas break in December 2009. Their reason for the rush? Perhaps I am mistaken; but the way I understood it, the reason behind the "push to pass" was *so they could avoid being influenced by their constituents when they went home for the holidays*.

What happened to <u>representing</u> your constituents? How inconsiderate! How arrogant! Who among us is willing to continue to support individuals who blatantly throw our "votes" in our faces and do what they please, regardless of what those who elected them believe and want?

Furthermore, some of the above-mentioned "servants of the people" were willing to risk being stranded in an impending storm, unable to get home to their families for Christmas day, to accomplish this "noble" feat. Who among us chooses to be represented by people who would opt to give up Christmas with their spouses, children, grandchildren, or parents so they are available in the country's capitol to manipulate the American people in such a ludicrous manner?

A few weeks later, there was discussion that if a Republican was elected to fill the late Senator Kennedy's vacant seat, his seating might be delayed so Massachusetts could not "influence" the vote on the health care bill, essentially leaving Massachusetts without this seat's vote during a critical time in American history.

Fortunately, when the dust settled, reason prevailed and it was concluded that purposely postponing the senator's seating – or rushing a vote to get it passed before he could be seated – would be a bad idea. Those who had proposed rushing the bill through finally concluded that it would be political suicide to do so, not just for themselves, but for their party as a whole.

But, why were they even <u>discussing</u> it? How did we get to this point? Why do we let them act this way? *What is wrong with <u>US</u> that we allow them to act this way, supposedly on OUR behalf?*

In February, 2010 in our own Washington state, the legislature took steps to override the Washington Taxpayer Protection Initiative (I-960), passed in 2007 by the citizens of Washington state, which requires the legislature to pass tax increases on the people by a two-thirds majority instead of a simple majority.

If the legislature can simply push a few buttons and override hard-fought taxpayer initiatives passed by the people, then why should the people ever bother to pass an initiative?

"They" say it is in our best interest and that they cannot wait until November for the taxpayers to agree to override the initiative themselves because of the "seriousness of the economic situation." I say, "Nonsense!"

Somehow, our elected officials believe that by raising taxes on people already struggling or suffering, they can improve our lives. I say, when they have made every cut they can and eliminated ALL of the "fat" of Washington state government services and expenditures (and your state, too), then we can talk about raising taxes. What an in-your-face insult to voters!

Get with it, people! Check their records and please do NOT re-elect any person who proposed, promoted, or voted for any such nonsense in any state in America! *If we continue to re-elect these people, who are so ready and willing to turn their backs on us, then we deserve what we get!* I do not think of myself as naive, but I was genuinely shocked upon hearing some of these news stories.

In April 2010, the nonsense in D.C. included a move to prohibit airlines from charging customers for carry-on bags that are placed in the overhead bins of airplanes. How in the world could this be an issue for the national legislature? Commerce will take care of itself. When people quit flying with the airlines because they will not pay extra for a carry-on bag, the airlines will have to rethink their fees.

Why do we allow Congress to waste time on issues regarding carry-on airline baggage? If this type of action falls within their responsibilities (I believe it does NOT), then why are they not, instead, writing a bill to keep insurance companies from paying a vendor $600+ for a $100 automobile windshield that takes less than 15 minutes to install? Hold a hearing on that! Is the legislature going to take on the issue of whether a taxi driver should provide more drink holders next?

And where on Earth do they get the "authority" to hold hearings questioning BP's involvement, or lack of it, in the release of the Lockerbie bombing convict?

Regardless of who was killed in the plane crash, how is that related to an oil spill investigation in 2010? This guy's release should have never been "negotiated" by anyone, anywhere. But, it is not the function of the United States legislature to question dealings of that type between people in other countries. Is it?

Do not elect or re-elect any person who cares more about special or corporate interests than about YOU and your family – and your business! Read their statements and study their records. Do your "homework."

And question anyone running for election to make sure they are willing to represent the people of their district, state, or country, ALL THE TIME – not whomever has the most money – or whenever they "feel like" representing you or anybody else.

Pay attention to what your elected officials really believe. Call them on important issues and convey to them what is unacceptable to you! Please!

Follow up on the campaign promises of people you voted for. Hold them accountable for their words! This is the only way we are ever going to be able to shovel our way out of our "too deep" political mess.

Civic duty – maybe it has always been about power, but I would like to think it was not always that way.

When Sarah Palin resigned as Governor of Alaska, I speculated to friends and relatives that she probably went into the governorship believing that she could actually DO something for the people of Alaska and, unfortunately for both her and Alaska, she got an unpleasant dose of reality over time. I cannot say that I agree with her decision to step down, but I am not in her shoes and do not know all of the circumstances and factors included in her decision-making process.

My personal belief is that Sarah thought any American citizen could dive into the political waters and make a difference. There was a time when I believed that, too. Her dose of reality cost her family much. That makes me genuinely sad. It is yet another disturbing reflection on our society sinking further into the mire – too deep to shovel. Or is it?

Unfortunately, "politics is politics." It is reassuring that Sarah is out working hard to get conservatives elected all across America. I believe she will, in at least some cases, be able to help positively influence the outcome of elections toward the conservative side of things and ultimately make a difference in the lives of Americans – *maybe on a wider scale than anybody else can.*

The presidency of the United States is a similar office. I have long held that it is much more important to carefully choose your U. S. Senators and Congressional Representatives than it is to choose a U.S. President. Congress really "runs the country."

The current President's failure to do all he promised in his campaign comes as no surprise. I believe, in his way, he was as naive as Sarah Palin as he stepped into the arena for the presidential election. That does not exempt him, however, from doing all he can to make America a better place for all of us and for future generations of American patriots. I have no direct knowledge of either his motives or his purposes in seeking the position he now holds.

The simple truth is that the President of the United States does not wield the kind of political power it takes to keep every campaign promise. "Politics as usual" will not change until we prohibit "career politicians" and return to the "citizen legislator."

WHERE DID ALL THE GOOD ONES GO?

My original intent was to write this subsection on "altruism"; however, after studying the origins of the word, I am not sure it is exactly the term I was seeking. In the sense that it is in opposition to "egotism," altruism is marginally appropriate in describing the selfless ethical attribute a candidate should possess to earn the votes of American patriots.

In the farming valley where I grew up, most of the local legislators early on were either farmers or lawyers. Whether it was correct or not, my perception always was that those were the only two groups of people who could afford to take off the time to meet and conduct the "business" of government for a few weeks each year.

During high school, I attended Idaho Youth Legislature both my junior and senior years (early 1970s). It was an enlightening and rewarding experience, serving on a committee and sitting in the marble chambers of the Idaho State Capitol building, enacting mock legislation.

In April 1973, then Governor, Cecil Andrus, wrote this in his introduction "TO THE OFFICERS AND MEMBERS OF THE 1973 IDAHO YOUTH LEGISLATURE": "Some of you may recall that in my Inaugural Address, I stated, 'It is time to speak out and insist that the enemy within is not the young of America. Rather, the enemy is many things: mismanagement of government and resources, disease, poverty, inadequate education, shrinking employment and other ills that afflict our society'."

Almost 40 years later, how are we doing on those issues, America? When are we going to get serious about "the enemy within"? How about NOW?

The purpose of the YMCA Youth and Government program, at least in the early 1970s when I was involved, was this: "To acquaint youth with the methods by which we, in our American form of democratic self-government, determine public policy

– that is – make our laws; and, to help them make practical application of Christian ideals to the problems of State Legislation."

The paragraph in the 1973 handbook entitled "Our Emphasis" says this: "The Youth and Government program of the YMCA is a project in Christian citizenship training, designed to bring to Idaho high school students a laboratory experience; by actual participation and understanding of the processes by which we make laws to govern our-selves. We seek to inspire youth legislators to develop Christian integrity and social responsibility as they think through some of the problems we face as a state, and to accept some responsibility for themselves for helping to solve these problems."

The General Chairman of the Idaho YMCA Youth and Government Committee at that time was Chief Justice Charles Donaldson, Idaho Supreme Court. Thank God for people like him and programs like this.

Although I never entered the political realm (and never will), I gained an increased awareness of how the American political system worked, through this program and through Syringa Girl's State, which I also attended in the summer following my junior year in high school. Programs like these are valuable in giving young people not only an understanding of how the legislative process works, but an interest and a desire to be a part of it at some future time.

We all know nobody is perfect. We cannot expect our citizen legislators to be perfect. What we CAN and SHOULD expect of them is SERVICE. They are elected to serve the people they represent. *They have no other function, either spelled out or implied.*

NEIGHBORS REPRESENTING NEIGHBORS

One of our neighbors – a man who was like a second father to me – ran for the state legislature when I was late into my high school years. I remember naively hoping he would not win. Why? Because most of what I had ever heard about politicians in the news involved reports of corruption, immorality, and lack of integrity.

This neighbor was a wonderful, compassionate, morally-upright, Christian man. My childish fear was that he would be somehow corrupted, or turned into something he was not, by serving in the legislature in the midst of the greed and corruption I perceived to be the "norm."

Looking back, it is plain to me that I should have perceived it as the "glass half full" and hoped that he could be a positive influence on any corrupt or immoral legislators he happened to rub elbows with. This individual would have been a true citizen legislator, elected to make the state where he lived, worked, and raised his family a better place for all.

I do not believe for one moment that there are not morally-upright, true citizen legislators among the members of the Senate and the House in our individual states and in Washington, D.C. There are many of them – and they are not all Republicans. But how often do we hear about the good ones? It seems that the news only pays attention when our citizen legislators have cheated on their wives, abused their power, or sold national secrets to the enemy.

Why doesn't one of the news networks do a profile every week for several <u>years</u> on those individuals who are standing firmly on moral high ground, representing their constituents in the way representation was intended to be done, and serving their state or country because they feel "called" to do so, not because they have something to gain personally or financially from their time in office?

Bring it on, media moguls! We are ready to be politically inspired!

JUST SAY "NO" TO CAREER POLITICIANS AND LOBBYISTS

[Influence, n. the capacity or power of persons or things to be a compelling force on or produce effects on the actions, behavior, opinions, etc., of others.] [1] *[Influence, (in'flü ans), 1. power of persons or things to act on others …]* [2] *[Influence. Power exerted over others …]* [3]

LOBBYISTS

Money spent on lobbyists in America today runs into the billions of dollars. Yes, that is BILLIONS! This concept did not originate with me, but I have to concur with those who believe there should be no such thing as a lobbyist – paid or otherwise. Lobbying has to go – it just has to GO. Period!

This messy issue really cannot be interpreted in any other way: companies and organizations who employ lobbyists are courting favors. The last I knew, "courting" resulted in marriage, in successful cases. Who is "marrying" whom? Who is "vowing to have and to hold" for richer or RICHER!? Why do we allow this courting of favors in 21st Century America? We have every right to say, "No, I do NOT take this ..."

There is no way that our senators and representatives can be expected to fairly represent their consituents with the endless stream of lobbyists begging and scratching for their "share" of the dollars to be dispensed or policies to be instituted that will favor a particular region, industry, business or organization.

With today's "information superhighway" and the instant communications we all have available to us, there is no reason for anyone to travel to a state capitol or to Washington, D.C. to ask for anything from the legislature in the 21st Century. Send them a text message or email and be done with it.

Influence peddling is a highly-developed professional skill in our 21st Century American society, and we need to not waste another moment before we begin the end of the lobbying system as it operates today. Get your shovel ready! We have a messy issue to bury.

There will be no fairness in the legislature until lobbying is extinct. It can have its place in the history books as the way NOT to operate government.

CAREER POLITICIANS

In my mind, there should never have been created the "beast" known as the "career politician." With some exceptions, most of our founding fathers were citizen legislators. Rather like doctors, preachers and teachers, they felt a "call" to serve. In the beginning, they served, they went home and took care of their families, homes, and businesses. It was not a "job." Each citizen legislator had a job that they left for a limited time to serve the people. Yes, many were (and are) lawyers. Legislation is law. [*Legislation, n. the act of making or enacting laws.*] [4]

Do you realize that what is commonly perceived to be the "benefit" of being represented by a "senior senator" or long-time representative is actually creating a huge gap between the "haves" and the "have nots" in terms of representation of the American taxpayers who elected them?

The "haves" would be those who are represented by an individual who has been in his or her seat long enough to be able to seriously influence other legislators and/or the President. The "have nots" would be those who are represented by someone new to the Washington political scene who has little or no influence.

Nobody can successfully convince me that a district or state with a "rookie" legislator in today's world is being equally represented in contrast to the district with a 20-year legislator – much less a 40-year legislator. *The taxpayers in two such districts are NOT being equally represented in any sense of the term!*

For this reason, and many others, there should be limits of two terms of two years each for ALL senators and representatives. There would be ZERO "senior senators." Everybody in the chambers would be on nearly equal footing; and maybe they would actually get something done for you and for me.

My Grandma Rose always said she never voted for an incumbent. Her belief was, if they had not "lined their pockets well enough the first time around," they did not deserve another chance. Now that I am middle aged, Grandma's political philosophy is even more amusing to me than it was when I was in my early twenties.

In addition, as I touched on in a previous sub-chapter, our legislatures, both state and national, are spending incredibly large amounts of time and resources on issues they have no business addressing. *It is our time and our money they are wasting.* How can anyone justify the legislature conducting hearings or writing a bill about carry-on baggage on airlines? This is not part of their "job description." Congress is exceeding the authority they have been given and many are purposefully abusing the power they are wielding over our lives (like discussing the delay of seating a new senator).

And we just sit and take it – year after year, term after term. I hope I heard wrong when I was told that just serving one term in the national legislature "entitles" a senator or representative to a generous, lifetime pension. This is not a career to retire from, and it is not a full-time "job." We cannot work a handful of years at our jobs and receive full pensions! Serving in the U. S. House or Senate is a call to serve the people for a time – not for a lifetime. What a crock!

We are trying to shovel our way out of a huge, stinky mire with a SPOON, America. *You can helplessly hang onto your spoon if you like, but my recommendation is that we hire an excavator!* I wonder if I can find one made in America.

LEFT AND RIGHT USUALLY FORM A WORKING PAIR

Most fairy tales begin with once upon a time ... Sometimes I feel like Americans today are living in a badly-written fairy tale. Partisanship has always existed, but it seems evident that the gap between "left" and "right" is steadily growing wider and wider.

The lack of bipartisanship in 21st Century America makes me think of the "Chevy guy" and the "Ford guy" attempting to have a reasonable discussion about the fine qualities of their autos. Few such reasonable discussions have ever taken place. I have always been amused by the immovability of the vehicle owner who is passionate about his or her favorite automobile. I have personally owned at least six "brands" of autos. (I started out with a Volkswagen bug like so many people my age did.) The handful of autos I have owned since 1974 cost me anywhere from $90 (yes, ninety dollars) to over $26,000; and I did not have any real problems with any of them, when you get right down to it.

So why do people argue so passionately about automobiles? *Apparently, we humans are not, by nature, bipartisan*.

Perhaps we need to remind ALL of our politicians that "left" and "right" usually make up a working pair. Try walking in shoes without one or the other – or working in gloves, minus one. How about the lenses in your glasses? How well do those work if the left and right are not perfectly coordinated?

There are exceptions, but isn't carrying a burden generally easier if you are using both your left and your right arms and hands? If your right front tire experiences a blowout, will the left one get you to your destination without its "partner"?

Try not hooking up both the left and right wires of an electric ceiling fan and see how many rotations it makes. You get the picture.

Now, how about insisting, not asking, that your elected representatives work TOGETHER to solve the messy issues threatening to choke the life out of our amazing country!

Recently, a fellow I know was talking about the concept of the government installing a water meter on a person's private well and charging the citizen for the water that comes out of the well.

As the owner of a VERY costly water well, I have to admit that I am not very receptive to the notion of this sort of government intervention into my life and finances. It is not like my family has an option to have something other than a well. We cannot even get the phone company to run DSL down our rural road. You know, in my lifetime, there will not ever be water lines from the city coming up to my mountain-side home six miles from town.

It is my understanding that there are counties in more than one state that are instituting this invasion into people's private property issues. At least one of them is in California.

When the government is willing to repay us the more than $25,000 we have invested in finding and pumping water and provide a written guarantee that it will continue flowing perpetually (which is always an unknown in the mountains, especially after an extended drought such as we have had in recent years) – and when they help us out with the power it takes to deliver the water 600' uphill to our home, and the expenses we incur keeping the pump and all of the related, sophisticated electronic well controls and pipe works functioning, then we may be able to discuss the possibility of *paying them to use our own water*. In the meantime, the topic is not even open for discussion!

It is coming – government intervention into more and more areas of our lives.

Government wants to control the local fruits and vegetables we buy from our neighbors at the farmer's market and tax the church for letting neighbors set up a canopy in the parking lot on Fridays.

We have to pay real money and wait for permission to cut down a handful of pine trees on our own land to clear a homesite and a driveway to get to it.

We cannot occupy our brand new custom-designed home until the county inspector has come by and performed an inspection prior to issuing an occupancy permit. *Permission to occupy ... our own home!*

Look out! Big brother might be about to graduate from knocking at your door to knocking it down!

A RUNAWAY TRAIN ON A BENT TRACK

Most conservative Americans today agree that government has grown too large for the common good. Disagreements exist between ultra-conservatives and moderates, but very few folks on the "right" think government should NOT be scaled back.

We cannot continue hurtling down this bent track without expecting a terrible crash in our future! Are you prepared for the crash? Or will you join me in attempting to fix the problem so the crash does not ever take place?

There are ideas rolling around in my head, but generating solutions for scaling back government is not among my gifts, so I will not attempt to provide detailed proposals. There was a promising news report about government accountability in Florida this year. Hopefully, there will be many, many more cities, counties and states that will be willing to jump on that "bandwagon" and show the taxpayers they can actually do something right.

My focus here will be to encourage those who DO have the gift of scaling back government to don their waders and get into the muck to help save America from the destruction that may very well be already on its way.

I never thought I would see this level of apathy in my lifetime. My day usually includes updating myself on local, national and global news items and listening to a variety of commentaries on current issues. I consider myself to be among the "well-informed" citizens of America. But, I still am surprised when I see some of the things that are happening from day to day around the country.

Our nation has been slipping further and further into "big government" for many decades as we have allowed the government to worm its way into more and more facets of our lives and our businesses.

Where we are today should not come as a total surprise to any of us, but I have to admit that I was stunned by the 2008 election results.

America, we must both straighten out the track <u>and</u> slow the train down. When we get it under control, we can turn it around and head back in the right direction, full speed ahead. If you think we cannot accomplish this, then you are not looking at the American citizens I am looking at.

We just need to get the tall boots and the shovels out and start using them – forthwith!

TAXATION WITHOUT WHAT?

Pardon me for sounding ignorant, but didn't we (Americans) used to consider taxation without representation a BAD thing? I cannot think of one reason why Americans would be tolerating it today. Enough with the apathy!

People, we cannot continue to allow those who have been elected "by the people" to ignore their constituents' wishes and do as they please – or carry out their decisions based upon the influence of lobbyists – to the detriment of our country and our people.

Entitlement and free country do not belong in the same sentence. An increasing sense of entitlement will eventually bankrupt our country and put us at the mercy of our enemies, both at home and abroad.

The percentages for voter turnout in our country are pathetic, at best. How can we expect a different outcome when so few people even participate in the democratic process? Pitiful ... we are pitiful!

Looking to the Future

- Are you not concerned about the chapter of history we are writing for our generation? Are we content to leave such a sorry legacy to our children and grandchildren? If not, what are we going to do about it – today?

- If Americans do not "put their foot down" and take back this country, then we do really deserve what we get. How about if you put your foot down on the top of your shovel blade and start digging!

- Is it "Tea Time"? Although I am supportive of the idea behind the "Tea Party" movement's efforts, and will remain hopeful that they can steer American politics back toward more conservative representation, I am cautious about the results for 2010 and 2012. We must be careful to not split the Republican party, thereby giving the Democrats a "leg up" in future elections. We have seen such a split happen before and the results were NOT pleasing to conservatives!

- This current "condition" of our great country is not what the founding fathers had in mind, I am sure.

MESSY ISSUE #3

ENERGY

ONE NATION, ON THE GRID, INDEFENSIBLE, WITH BATTERIES AND NUKE WASTE FOR ALL

Energy in America is a messy issue because, let's face it, there is no existing "patch" or "pill" to wean us off of oil. And we cannot quit it "cold turkey." Even if you take personal automobiles out of the picture altogether, electricity production, manufacturing and cargo transportation consume much of the fossil fuels used worldwide.

Not exploring and developing every available, morally-correct solution for energy in the U.S. should NOT be an option for the American people. We must explore all avenues open to us.

If the "activists" circumnavigating the globe protesting against oil and coal development truly are interested in saving the environment, why does their new mega-yacht have a helipad (now <u>there</u> is an energy-efficient mode of transportation), room for "a flotilla of inflatable rafts and small dinghies," (perhaps made with PVC and powered by what?) and backup diesel engines? This will be the sixth vessel in their fleet.[5] Hopefully, their generators are solar powered. Is the satellite system for streaming live video worldwide from the ship made of renewable resources? That is probably solar powered, too, right? How about those mega masts for their mega sails? What are they made of? As far as that goes, what are the sails made of? Of course they will not be petroleum based nylon. They have a lofty goal to use the backup engines only 10% of the time, but what is the reality on a trip to New Zealand or Japan?

Perhaps, instead of floating and flying around the entire planet burning up fossil fuels, they could stay home doing something else with their lives, like coming up with REAL solutions to our environmental problems.

You know environmentalists drive cars and trucks. You know they jet here and there to pursue their "cause." They have even had to beg fuel from the oil companies when they ran low in the past.

And beyond the fuel they are perhaps wasting, I can almost guarantee you that in their quest to "save the environment," many environmental activists use most, if not all of the 40+ items on the following list:

- Antifreeze
- Bearing grease
- Boats
- Cameras
- Carpeting
- CDs and DVDs
- Credit cards
- Deck shoes
- Detergents
- Diesel fuel
- Electrical tape
- Epoxy paint
- Fan belts
- Hoses
- Ice chests or refrigerators
- Insect repellant
- Life jackets
- Lip balm

- Marine and automotive batteries
- Medicines
- Motor oil
- Nylon rope
- Oil filters
- Paddles
- Permanent press clothes
- Plastic bags
- Plastic cups and tableware
- Plexiglass
- Raincoats
- Safety glass
- Shampoo
- Solvents
- Sunglasses
- Sunblock
- Telephones
- "Tennis shoes"
- Tires
- Toilet seats
- Tool boxes
- Toothbrushes
- Upholstery
- Water pipes
- Waterproof boots
- Wire insulation
- Zippers

And that is just the beginning of the list of several hundred items most of us in 21st Century America (including environmental activists) use on a pretty-much daily basis. Even one of my shovel handles is made of plastic, and the barn boots in the picture on the cover of this book are undoubtedly made from something not renewable.

I don't know about you, but I like having everything I could possibly want on the store shelves in every store I walk into. Do I NEED that? No. Do I like it? Sure! Does it cost us all something to have those items on the store shelves 24/7/365? Yes!

So how do the items get onto the store shelves and into the coolers and freezers? It is not magic, people; and it is not rocket science. Everything you find in the store, including the store, itself – parking lot, building, flooring, paint, shelves and lighting – is transported in planes, trains, cargo ships and trucks.

It is difficult for me to picture electric tractor-trailer rigs climbing over snowy mountain passes hauling their burdens from coast to coast. Trains move a lot of freight in many areas of the nation, including through our small town; but they do not go everywhere; and there certainly is not a train track next to every store parking lot (although it is only two blocks away from most stores in our little town).

Americans want every new product on the shelf – *right next to all of their old favorites* – as soon as it appears in a television ad! The stores get bigger; the electricity and heating/cooling bills get higher; the truck, train, plane and marine shipping required to have every product on the shelf every day increases, and increases, and increases.

Have you met anyone this week who is willing to give up having everything on the shelf every day – at the grocery store? at the auto parts store? at the car stereo shop? at the drug store? at the office supply store? at the furniture store? at the "big box" store that has groceries, auto parts, car stereos, pharmaceuticals, office supplies and furniture all in the same store? I have not met any such person in my circle of friends, co-workers, relatives and acquaintances.

Who among us is willing to ban airplanes? Do you want the airlines to offer flights every hour, everywhere, for your convenience? Are you willing to request that they drop their schedules back to twice a day everywhere they fly? Maybe even once a day? Are airplanes ever going to use electricity to get from Airport A to Airport B? Are they going to use solar panels? Are they going to use nuclear fuel? Do you know how many jet airplanes leave the ground every day worldwide?

Do you know how much fuel, of all types, the U.S. Government uses? The Air Force? The Navy? The Marines? The Army? The Coast Guard? The National Guard? NOAA? NASA? The President and his entourage? Congress?

Did you know that cruise ships travel about one foot per gallon? That is what I heard. Oh, that is different, you say? We should not count cruise ships when we are looking at ways to save our planet?

If nothing else, for the short term, we could be creating many well-paying jobs for Americans by developing all of the oil we DO have – and yes, including ANWR. Based on the long-term success on the North Slope, the FACTS prove that there is little to no additional risk to developing our oil resources in the miniscule spot on the Alaska map that is the fraction of the Arctic National Wildlife Refuge proposed to produce oil. *Get the real facts, folks!*

Every single dime that goes to a foreign nation for oil (or any other resource we have available but are not developing in our own country) is an insult to American workers, especially those who are un-employed or under-employed.

Are there people in Saudia Arabia, Venezuela, and Iran losing their homes because they cannot pay for them due to lack of a job that will support their family? Even if there are, should we consider their people before our people?

How about if, to save energy costs, we close all the stores and businesses at night and have curfews like in the "good old days"? Think how much electricity and fuel that would save! That would be ok with me from a purely simplistic standpoint – I seldom leave home after 10 p.m. for any reason; and it would keep most of the hoodlums off the streets at night.

But, if we closed down all the businesses at night, look how many people would be out of work. High-rise towers across America are not lit up at night because the execs are working (for the most part), they are lit up because the cleaning and maintenance crews are working at night.

Maybe we need to rotate work schedules so a block of offices is closed on a particular morning for two hours for cleaning and maintenance, rather than at night. It's just a thought ...

Our Addiction to Plastic

Yeah, we're addicts – we're hooked – we are in so deep we will probably never be able to shovel our way out of this one. Maybe not every one of us, but most of us are "hooked on plastic."

Just look around you. Oh, don't worry, you don't have to look far. There are probably numerous plastic or other petrochemical-based computer hardware items on your desk. There might be a plastic thermal coffee cup by your plastic mouse, next to your plastic-trimmed PC tower, your plastic monitor, your plastic printer, and your plastic speakers. The door and drawer handles on your desk might be plastic, painted gold or silver. I wrote much of this book using a plastic-housed laptop. I was looking around MY office (and typing on my plastic keyboard) when I wrote the list I just named.

There are probably plastic wheels on the plastic legs of your office chair. Your stapler might be plastic, and your cellophane tape dispenser (plus the tape in it) and pencil sharpener are almost undoubtedly plastic. The casings on your ink pens and mechanical pencils are likely plastic, along with the desk "organizer" where they spend most of their time. I did see some ink pen housings made from recycled cardboard recently. Great idea, as long as it does not take extra fuel to recycle the cardboard.

Your adding machine or calculator(s), desk phone, and desk lamp are probably plastic or some form of composite, too.

In your kitchen, your coffee maker, espresso machine, toaster, breadmaker, ice cream machine, blender, food processor and many of your drinking glasses are probably plastic, along with the hinge covers and ventillation grills on your refrigerator (and the bins and compartments inside it). The racks in your deep-freeze and dishwasher are more than likely coated in petroleum-related products. If it is fairly new, the petroleum-dependent safety glass shelves in your refrigerator are bordered in plastic trim.

I am going to venture a guess that your CD alarm clock, camera(s), parts of your tripod, and your camera charger are also plastic. Your cell phone(s), the chargers for your cell phone (both the car one and the AC one), and your home phones (four or five of them in most houses) are probably plastic products.

The cords that connect the phone and your computer to the wall are also plastic coated. The satellite internet modem and wireless router on top of my desk hutch are both plastic. There are at least four plastic alarm clocks in my home.

Count the plastic CDs and DVDs in plastic cases in your house and car(s). Count the plastic forks, knives, and spoons in your picnic set. Count the plastic clothes hangers in your closet, and the cosmetics and shampoos in plastic bottles in your bathrooms. Do you have more than a handful of cleaning products under any of your sinks that are in something other than plastic containers? Even if you use cloth bags for grocery shopping, do you use anything besides plastic bags in your garbage cans?

Count the cords and plugs on every item that is plugged into an outlet in your house. They are plastic, as are the covers for the electric receptacles you plug them in to and the coatings on the wires that feed the outlets. Unless they are oak, your light switch covers (and the switches, themselves) are probably plastic – in every room in your house and garage. How about your garage door opener and its remote control? Are those plastic?

Do you have wonderful, washable vinyl paint on your walls? Do you know where that comes from? Is there vinyl or laminate flooring or nylon carpet on your floors? Do your washer and dryer have many plastic parts?

How about polyester fabrics in your clothing? Are they in your car, too? Did you know there are coal products in your polyester fabrics, as well? Do you own any shoes or boots with soles that are made of anything other than non-renewable products?

Look in your kitchen cabinets and count the food storage containers, drink pitchers, serving bowls, and other items that are made of plastic. Do you have a plastic garlic press, vegetable chopper, or potato peeler? If they are not wood, what are the handles on your knife set and steak knives made out of? Are your measuring cups and measuring spoons plastic? How about your electric mixer? Even my food dehydrator is all plastic except the heat element; and my bread-maker is housed in plastic.

How about multiple television sets (with plastic remotes), stereo components (with plastic remotes), VCRs (with plastic remotes), DVD players (with plastic remotes), portable fans, boom boxes, smoke detectors, and the knobs on your appliances? Does your house contain video game systems (and games) and boxes and (plastic) bins of plastic toys? In fact, you may very well have plastic bins and containers in every room in the house. And garage. And poolhouse. And greenhouse. I have one in the back of my car to house emergency supplies. Do you?

I don't know about yours, but my home gym, ski machine and stepper came with plastic parts. Do you have plastic chairs and tables on your patio? I do.

Do you, or any members of your family, use disposable shaving razors? If you use bottled water, count the bottles you have used today, this month, this year. Now there is one thing I do NOT use. Praise God for the wonderful well water we have and the glass bottles we carry it around in when we need to take it with us.

Most of the desks in most of the offices at the public school where I work are made entirely of or contain plastic, along with many of the storage cabinets and all of the student desks, tables and chairs (which are part metal and part plastic products).

Is there anything in your car, pickup or SUV, including the frame, that is NOT made out of non-renewable resources?

So let's do a reality check. What kind of trees do they use to make all of the items in this list of plastic-related products we use that barely touches the surface? Ummmm ... We all know the answer is NONE – most of them come from petroleum and/or coal.

The issue of plastic is not officially related to "energy" except that it is related to petroleum, but it seemed to logically fit in this chapter. Many of those calling for changes in our energy policies fail to recognize the heavy impact on worldwide petroleum production the manufacture and shipment of plastics creates. Changing auto fuel will not get us out of producing and shipping petroleum around the globe.

Beyond their "plasticness," many of the items named in the previous pages also emit toxins into the air of your home, car and office. Wow, great idea! Make virtually everything out of plastic, and import most of it from China where they have no interest in whether we overflow our landfills and breathe toxic air all day every day.

Fill our offices, homes, automobiles and stores with formaldehyde and other toxins breaking out of plastic and rubber so we breathe it everywhere we spend time. And then wonder why our kids have syndromes and disorders we never heard of a few decades ago and why we are dying of cancer or sick all the time.

As an asthmatic, I can barely walk around in most of the "big box" stores because the fumes breaking out of the plastics and composites throughout these stores cause me to develop an instant headache and difficulty breathing.

Frankly, I do not see how people work in those places. I can barely stay inside long enough to purchase what I need and get out! OSHA should really look into that. There are going to be some serious, long-term consequences of making people work in such a potentially toxic environment, I believe.

Personally, I would like to see the inside of Al Gore's house – his pantry, his refrigerator, his closets, his garage. Are the hangers in his closets made of TREES or PETROLEUM or METAL? Maybe they are made out of recycled cardboard. *Recycled cardboard clothes hangers might be a really good idea. Someone should look into that.* Maybe Al Gore can earn his next Nobel prize for making recycled cardboard clothes hangers.

WHO IS GOING TO FEED ME WHILE THE TRUCKS AND PLANES AND SHIPS ARE EATING MY CEREAL AND CHIPS?

Spend even a little time on America's interstate highways and you can have no doubt that shipping freight via semi trucks is using a huge amount of fuel in 21st Century America. Check the ports full of cargo ships and the airports that are full of cargo planes, literally around the clock. The numbers are staggering!

A "biodiesel" alternative fuel for cargo shippers is a worthy idea. But, if we grow our fuel, who will grow our food? An increasing number of states have issued mandates on either production or usage of biodiesel and ethanol.

There will even be some trials using biofuels in jet airplanes in the near future. America burns a LOT of jet fuel every year. Is it feasible to think that we can replace all of that fuel with biofuels?

Whatever we choose to do, we absolutely must ensure that growing our fuel does not increase our reliance upon foreign nations for purchase of our everyday food needs or raise the price of food items so drastically that the average citizen cannot afford to purchase them.

We must NOT restrict ourselves on our ability to produce reasonably-priced foods for our citizens (and for our livestock) by committing too much of our growing capacity to fuel sources. *It would be very foolish to allow ourselves to be any more vulnerable than we already are in the area of feeding ourselves.*

Some of the fields in our little farming valley are planted in grain this year, rather than the usual alfalfa. Maybe it has something to do with the new biofuel plant going in south of us – and maybe it does not. I do know that if less farmers grow alfalfa, we can expect the price of alfalfa to take a leap up. The cost of both meat (including chicken, pork and beef) and milk could escalate because of a major change in who is growing what, where. Nothing is without cause and effect – and consequences – in our world today.

Growing algae for alternative fuel sounds interesting and promising. It would seem unlikely that such a venture would be undertaken on existing farm land or take our farming resources away from feeding our country's people and livestock. Creating algae "farms" in states where the growing conditions are appropriate sounds like a potentially good economic boost, if the fuel is affordable without the American taxpayers subsidizing it.

There has been talk of a particular kind of grass that grows quickly, almost anywhere, that can be used to make fuel. As long as that would not take up ranch lands where cattle currently graze, or cost too much to transport to a "refinery," that "fuel source" is probably worth seriously pursuing.

The plant waste from harvesting and processing crops should be a viable source of "bio" materials, as long as trucking it to a fuel-production facility does not consume more fuel than the facility creates. Distilling of crops like mint and hops, along with others, leaves mass quantities of "refuse."

Fuels made from wood products are also being produced now. Given the restrictions on logging that have shut down the mills, parked the logging trucks, and devastated the economy in logging communities where I live, I do not see how this can be a viable solution that will have any real impact on our use of fossil fuels nationwide. Loggers are forced to drive four hours each way, at times, to pick up logs for the lumber mills in our part of the country now. How far they will have to truck wood waste from its source to a biofuel plant must be carefully considered.

If we use a lot of wood waste for production of alternative fuels, will there be a shortage of particle board and plywood – or will it suddenly cost $100 per sheet? Will the price of pellets for your pellet stove double overnight? Can they make biofuel out of spotted owl droppings? Maybe they could burn those in pellet stoves ...

We absolutely should encourage research and development of responsible alternative fuel sources. I do not even have a problem with the government providing some R & D grants for this activity as long as the use of the funds is carefully monitored and the funds do not go to some senator's brother-in-law who does not know a thing about what he is "researching."

In reality, the bottom line is this: biodiesel is still diesel fuel, regardless of what organic substance is used to produce it.

BUY LOCAL – SAVE FUEL

Admittedly, I am as guilty as anyone of purchasing food items that come from other countries, although our family is attempting to buy locally as much as possible. Do you have any idea what it costs to transport fresh fruits and vegetables to your local supermarket or neighborhood grocery store from Australia, New Zealand and Brazil? Or from California to New York? Or from Florida to Washington State? From Texas to Minnesota?

My family is blessed to be able to purchase eggs from chickens that live just a few miles away and are not fed any hormones or chemicals. We also buy locally-grown beef products packaged by members of our community who care what goes into our food.

Purchasing items that are produced locally reduces consumption of fuel because it takes the transportation element almost completely out of the picture. So "buy local" is not just good for the local business community, it is good for the environment.

We all realize that not every community has the capability to grow food for its citizens; although, I believe there must be ways even inner-city communities, if they so choose, could use rooftop gardens and every vacant lot that is not being used for something else to grow food for their neighbors. Why aren't we doing more of that nationwide? Our government is DISCOURAGING, not encouraging, local farmer's markets that have sprung up across the country. What is not smart about taking the transportation element out of our food supply to save fuel?

ELECTRIC TRAINS RUN AROUND THE BASE OF THE CHRISTMAS TREE

It is wonderful that they are designing vehicles that use alternative forms of energy. In the past, efforts to do so have been purposely undermined, at times. This is unfortunate, because we could already be way ahead of where we are in decreasing our burning of fossil fuels. Now, if they will just come up with a reasonably-priced, seriously fuel efficient, "true-crawler" four-wheel-drive SUV that will get up my driveway in the winter!

There is reason for concern, however, about all of America's cars and trucks being powered by batteries and electricity. Electric cars, trucks and forklifts require banks of batteries, and battery waste in our country concerns me very much. We already use an incredible amount of batteries in America, including in battery-operated tools, electronics, and smoke alarms. And that is just for the average American home consumer – it does not take into account commerical use of batteries nationwide.

Even if battery waste is housed in a "toxic waste facility," it still concerns me. I do not know that there is much we can do about toxic battery waste, OR the use of petroleum products to create the batteries in the first place, in our already battery-dependent society. Someone should look into that ...

ALL of the goods and services that most people believe they cannot do without for even a day or two are transported by planes and trucks and trains and ships. The likelihood of any of these cargo-shipping sources, nationwide, being powered by electricity for the long-term seems remote.

As I mentioned previously, we all want to walk into the store and find every item we can think of on the shelf, in the refrigerated sections, and in the freezers – ready for us to purchase and take home. We want fresh fruits and vegetables in all four seasons of the year in all parts of the country. We want 47 choices of shampoo, 20 flavors of yogurt, and 30 kinds of BBQ sauce (all in plastic) to choose from.

There is a price to pay for this "convenience," folks; and it is unlikely that this "price" will change significantly with switching to an alternate form of energy for producing and delivering it to your neighborhood store or area "big box" merchant.

Electric trains are feasible in some cities. In fact, electric trains have been used in some cities since electric transmission lines have been in existence. Based on what I know about their practicality (or lack of it) as a solution for freight hauling from coast to coast, however, they are not a likely solution for wide-spread use. Many former rail beds across the country have been converted (probably with Federal assistance) to wonderful bike and hiking trails because they were no longer in use.

Where there are electric trains, there must be electric transmission lines. And it seems to me like the last arguments I heard against using wind generators for widespread power production involved environmentalists waging war against building more electrical transmission lines across America.

Even if increasing the number of electric-powered trains across America is a feasible solution, the electricity we use is not self-generating. It all comes from <u>somewhere</u>. Unless it is produced by

84

moving water or air, there is a non-renewable resource cost to all electricity use, including solar panels and solar storage batteries.

If electric trains are to get out from under the Christmas tree and into our daily lives in a significant way, there will have to be environmentalists willing to make concessions on construction of transmission lines and rails. This potential solution is not without many issues, both environmental and financial, that would need to be resolved for it to succeed.

CAN YOU SAY VULNERABLE? THE DANGERS OF A ONE-NATION GRID

We have already determined that electric autos are potentially a good idea. However, do we really have enough electricity to charge all of the cars in America daily? Somehow, I do not think so.

Are we going to have to schedule our car charging like some city dwellers have to schedule watering their lawns? What if you have to get to work and it is "not your day"? Are people going to ultimately end up breaking the law to charge their cars so they can work and support their families?

What if the cost of electricity triples and we cannot afford to charge up our cars at all? Have you considered that? Will you have any control over that?

The idea of tying the entire nation into a single electric grid is extremely frightening to me, for more than one reason. Having seen the results of over-usage outages in the "minimal" nine-state grid in the western American states, I am very leery about trying to put together a national power grid. Obviously, Alaska and Hawaii would not even be able to be included in a U. S. "national power grid."

The most serious power outages ever in my area of the country were during the hottest months of the year when some people need their air conditioning to keep ALIVE. We have created hundreds of thousands of multi-story living spaces nationwide, where the windows do not even open so a person COULD get fresh air if they needed it to stay alive without the building's air-handling system in operation.

"Blowing the grid" is already a serious and real risk to health and safety for many Americans. And a city without electricity for its stoplights is a nightmare, extraordinare! Every intersection becomes a four-way stop "sign." Bad news for all involved. Been there, done that – don't want to do it often.

Mega-cities could not even begin to cope with traffic if the electrically - and electronically-operated traffic signal lights were not in operation. Just look back at the news reports from the disaster in the Eastern States in August of 2003, then picture that from coast to coast and from Canada to Mexico!

Imagine the crime spree that would ensue, following an extended power outage anywhere in the U.S. We would be very unwise to leave ourselves in such a vulnerable position EVER in the future.

Looking at this issue from a national-security standpoint, questioning the advisability of a one-nation grid is not paranoia, it is prudence in light of the vulnerability to sabotage that would become reality with such a wide-spread grid. *A national electric grid would be vulnerable to both international and domestic terrorists.*

Realistically, can we even produce and deliver enough electricity to power millions of cars? Will we have to install plug-in meters downtown so people who drive in from the suburbs can charge their cars up before they drive back home? Will people just swipe their debit card or electric utility charge card and "juice up" while they shop? Has anybody done studies on what would happen to the electric grids in our country if we all were driving electric cars and all plugged them in when we got home from work (or got TO work)?

What means are we going to use to create that much electricity? Will that require increased dependence on fossil fuels, or create nuclear or coal waste to be "disposed of"?

What a monster we have created with our energy consumption in America! I am not sure our boots are tall enough or our shovels big enough to handle this issue, either. It will take all of the ingenuity and resources of the American people to solve this problem for the long-term.

ENERGY INDEPENDENT ... REALLY?

Like it or not, America has allowed herself to become far too dependent on fossil fuels, in general, and on foreign oil, in particular. It simply is not feasible to think we can continue to consume energy as we are consuming it today, regardless of the source of the energy.

And, as we insist on continuing to "help" third-world countries to industrialize and "develop," the world's consumption of all forms of energy will continue to increase exponentially. You think we are using a lot of petroleum and plastic now? Just wait until every nation on Earth is as developed as we are!

The global track record for environmental responsibility is not stellar, by any means. Even if we solve all of our own "in-house" energy and environmental issues, the average American patriot will have little or no control over world-wide energy consumption or environmental disasters in the foreseeable future – or of foreign countries polluting the atmosphere we all share at levels the U.S. will not allow.

What are the consequences to American patriots of NOT becoming energy independent?

LOOKING TO THE FUTURE

- WE CANNOT GO BACKWARD. WE HAVE TO GO FORWARD.

- SOME PEOPLE WHO ARE COMING UP WITH REAL ENERGY SOLUTIONS ARE HAVING TO TAKE THEM OUTSIDE OUR OWN COUNTRY TO DEVELOP THEM. THAT DOES NOT MAKE ANY SENSE AT ALL FOR AMERICA! STOP THAT!

- WHETHER OR NOT AMERICANS SCALE BACK ON ENERGY CONSUMPTION AND DEVELOP ALTERNATIVE ENERGY SOLUTIONS, THE WHOLE WORLD WILL CONTINUE TO BE IMPACTED (BOTH ECONOMICALLY AND ENVIRON-MENTALLY) BY OIL PRODUCTION FOR MANY GENERATIONS TO COME.

- WE ARE CAPABLE OF LEARNING OUR LESSONS AND TAKING STEPS TO FIND REAL SOLUTIONS. WHAT IS PREVENTING US FROM JUST DOING IT? LET'S START WITH A NATURAL GAS PIPELINE FROM ALASKA TO THE LOWER 48! NOW THERE ARE SOME WELL-PAYING JOBS.

- IF THE GOVERNMENT OPERATES A NATION-WIDE ELECTRIC GRID, IT WILL SURELY BE THE END OF FREE ENTERPRISE IN THE PRODUCTION OF ELECTRICITY — THE LOCAL ELECTRIC COMPANY WILL BE THE NEXT TO APPEAR ON THE "ENDANGERED SPECIES" LIST.

MESSY ISSUE #4

GLOBAL WARMING

OCCUPYING A SELF-REGULATING PLANET

GLOBAL WARMING, GLOBAL COOLING, WHO'S TO KNOW? AS FOR ME, I'M GLAD THE 1,000' THICK ICE SHEET IS GONE

©2009gjJones

It might sound far-fetched to those who want to blame it all on human activity, but I am pretty confident Planet Earth has been warming steadily on its own since the last ice age. Climate change is a fact of life.

The river valley where I live (pictured above) was almost undoubtedly carved by a glacier. Those who know more than I do about it theorize that a slab of ice called a Cordilleran Ice Sheet covered this area up to 1,000' thick at some time in the distant past. It is reasonable to assume that a warming trend caused this ice sheet to melt quite some time ago. Whether the demise of the ice was fast or slow is speculated, but not provable. But it melted – all of it.

There is much physical evidence that a glacier moved through here. I cannot think of any other explanation for the round river rock lying on the ground more than ¼ mile up the mountain from the valley floor, near the top of our property.

Obviously, if the ice sheet had not melted, this would not be a beautiful valley with farms on the valley floor and forests on the mountainsides. Frankly, I like it this way better. In fact, I think I can safely assert that everyone who lives in this valley likes it better with the mega ice sheet gone.

How much humans contribute to the warming of the globe is debatable. *That we contribute is not an issue – we undoubtedly contribute in a variety of ways.* It is ridiculous to suggest, however, that any-thing we infinitesimal humans can do will permanently stop the planet from continuing to regulate itself.

BLASTING, STEAMING AND SPEWING OUR WAY TO A WARMER PLANET

When the Mt. Redoubt volcano was spewing ash all over the Kenai Peninsula in Alaska during the winter of 1989-1990, scientists informed us that one eruption of this one volcano produced more ozone-effecting material than all of the many petrochemical facilities in the area could <u>ever</u> produce. Unless my memory fails me, we had ashfall from nine volcanic eruptions in just that one winter.

Because there are volcanic eruptions worldwide repeatedly blasting, steaming, and spewing away on virtually every continent – in Hawaii there is red-hot bubbling lava spilling into the ocean 24/7/365 – it only makes sense that volcanoes, even today, have a significant impact on global warming. There is no way that documented eruptions under the ocean and lava rivers flowing continuously into the ocean can NOT be changing the temperature of the oceans. With the passage of time, this HAS to have an impact on the temperature of the oceans and, therefore, on the temperature of the planet – and, yes, perhaps even an impact on where ocean fish live and travel.

There is no way that ash and steam from sometimes multiple volcanoes worldwide, rising into the atmosphere circling the globe month after month, year after year does NOT impact the ozone layer.

If you are interested, information on daily volcanic activity, both new and ongoing, can be found online at http://www.volcano.si.edu/reports/usgs/ or by searching online for "daily Earth volcanic eruptions." It is clear to me that volcanic activity is contributing greatly to global warming, both warming the oceans and impacting the ozone layer.

Add hydrothermal vents, some of which are 400º C (that's 752º F), including at least nine under the Arctic Ocean[6], to the picture; and it is even more unlikely that the oceans are not naturally warming. When was the last time your neighbor tried to ruin our planet by firing up a hydrothermal vent in the ocean or a volcano in Iceland?

Do the people complaining about the polar bears' ice floes getting smaller and smaller discuss the hydrothermal vents under the Arctic Ocean? Not that I have noticed. Do they talk about the impact the tour vehicles carrying tourists for "up close and personal" encounters out among the polar bears may have on the bears' breeding and reproduction patterns? *Surely they would not omit factors that important. I probably missed something* ... Are those tour vehicles burning diesel or gasoline fuel?

TROPICAL-REDWOOD DESERT? HUH?

In my closet is a huge fishing tackle box containing an assortment of dinosaur fossils – collected in the New Mexico desert in the 1950s – that obviously came into existence a very long time ago while that area was speculated to have been a tropical rain forest. I seriously doubt that mankind had anything at all to do with the transition from rain forest to desert in New Mexico, either before or after the fossils in my case were formed.

When I was a child, my dad "harvested" part of a petrified redwood stump in the Owyhee desert. I remember him saying the stump was about 12' across. Hmmmm ... the area is currently covered by sagebrush and horned toads and rocks and dead grass and it once had redwood trees whose trunks were 12' across; but they have been gone so long their stumps have turned to stone. How ridiculous would it be to believe that mankind had anything to do with the transition from redwood forest to desert in that case, either?

Washington state, where I live, has some of the most telling and compelling evidence of long-term climate change available for examination right on the land surface – a lot of it right smack in the middle of the state. My husband and I have a fascinating and varied selection of it in the rock gardens that grace our front yard. We live in a radically-changed climate.

IDENTIFYING THE RESPONSIBLE PARTY

We acknowledge that we, as individuals, as a society and as a country, should be as environmentally responsible as practically and financially possible; but we also recognize that what we mere humans do (or do not do) will, unfortunately, have a limited impact on the long-term condition of this planet we temporarily occupy.

Climate change is going to be a fact of life for generations far beyond our own. It is critical that we get the true facts and share them with the next generation. Each and every one of us must realize that we can have a limited role in keeping our planet in the best shape it can be in while we occupy it. *We also have to acknowledge that there are going to be many aspects of environmental change that will not ever be within our control.* We cannot shut off geothermal vents and volcanoes. We cannot control the effects of ash clouds on global weather and precipitation.

Ongoing volcanic activity in Hawaii continues to consume homes and land and warm the ocean water. Not one single person on Earth has the power to do anything about it. There is no "responsible party" in the volcanic environmental disaster in Hawaii.

The recent volcanic activity in Iceland is going to give us a very clear picture of the total devastation of an environment by events and circumstances completely beyond any control of the local residents who have been literally buried in ash. Words can hardly describe it. It will be interesting to see what the long-term effects of this ash blanket will be on livestock, farm crops, human health, and Iceland's national economy.

Will it become evident, eventually, that the record-breaking heat on one side of the planet and the record-breaking flooding on the other through the summer of 2010 were, in part, a result of the Icelandic ash clouds? A little time will tell ...

There is no "responsible" party in Iceland's volcanic disaster, either. It is not logical to think that there is anything anybody could have done to prepare for such a serious environmental event. But much can be learned in the aftermath.

And we can rest assured that other similar natural environmental disasters will take place on Planet Earth as years and generations pass.

It's Not All About Money ... Is It?

Our globe has been warming steadily since the last time it was covered with ice. And even if there really was not an "ice age" and the transformation of the valley I live in was caused by Noah's flood, man's role in this messy issue is still infinitessimal, to say the least. Global warming appears to be very "big business." In its own way, that is incredibly sad and tragic.

It is also sad that the world's glaciers are melting and people will not be able to "enjoy" visiting them at some time in the future if they completely disappear. Life on Planet Earth is not always fair.

It is more sad that villages in some parts of the world are facing the necessity of finding another source of life-giving water besides the streams coming from the melting glaciers once they are completely gone (although the glaciers may actually rebuild themselves at some point). Maybe those people will have to eventually drill wells like the rest of us. Who knows? It is within the realm of possibility, anyway.

LOOKING TO THE FUTURE

- WE CANNOT THROW UP OUR HANDS AND SAY, "THERE IS NOTHING TO BE DONE," HOWEVER, WE MUST WEIGH OUR OPTIONS AND OUR ACTIONS IN LIGHT OF THE ECONOMIC AND SOCIAL IMPACT OUR SOLUTIONS WILL HAVE ON AMERICA'S CITIZENS, BOTH IN THE SHORT TERM AND IN THE LONG TERM.

- WE NEED TO QUIT ALLOWING THOSE WISHING TO FINANCIALLY CAPITALIZE ON THE "ISSUE" OF GLOBAL WARMING TO DO SO AT OUR EXPENSE. ENOUGH, ALREADY!

- WE MUST CONTINUE TO DO WHAT IS WITHIN OUR POWER TO PROTECT OUR PLANET, WITHOUT GOING TO EXTREMES.

- WE MUST EMBRACE THE REALITY THAT CLIMATE CHANGE WILL CONTINUE TO TAKE PLACE AS IT HAS SINCE THE BEGINNING OF TIME.

MESSY ISSUE #5

FAMILY VALUES

CIVILIZATION IS GONE TO RUIN

RIGHTEOUSNESS EXALTS A NATION,
BUT SIN IS A DISGRACE TO ANY PEOPLE.

PROVERBS 14:34

Why is "family values" a messy issue? Because our society continues to become more and more "uncivilized" and degrade more and more toward chaos and anarchy because our core values are being muted and muddled, in part by an absence of a male and a female, who are married to each other, in a two-parent household, with the man as the spiritual head of the house. Daily news reports document again and again the very clear reality that we are becoming LESS, not more civilized as time passes.

Thus says the LORD, "Stand by the ways and see and ask for the ancient paths, where the good way is, and walk in it; and you will find rest for your souls. But they said, 'We will not walk in it.' And I set watchmen over you, saying, 'Listen to the sound of the trumpet!' But they said, 'We will not listen.'

Therefore hear, O nations, and know, O congregation, what is among them. Hear, O Earth: behold, I am bringing disaster on this people, the fruit of their plans, because they have not listened to My words, and as for My law, they have rejected it also."
Jeremiah 6:16-19 NASB

The God of the Bible has a well-documented, long-term track record of showing people His displeasure when He has had enough of their disrespect and rejection. America, we are truly reaping what we have sown.

It was my privilege to grow up in a small, Western U.S. town where the public grade school principal prayed over the intercom every morning and we sang patriotic songs in the classroom, with our teacher enthusiastically and sincerely pounding out the music on the piano that was in virtually every grade school classroom in every small town at that time.

In 21st Century America, there are schools where the number of students with gunshot wounds is in triple digits every year. What a dramatic difference.

A DIFFERENT WORLD

I really do understand that we live in a "different world" today. But a lot of our country's (and our society's) problems could be solved by a return to the family as it was when I grew up and the values that were the "norm" as recently as 30 years ago.

This is not to say that couples did not get divorced or teenage girls did not get pregnant out of wedlock or priests did not molest little boys when I was growing up. It was not a perfect world then, either. But, at least we had a clear vision of what was right and wrong and pretty much everybody was "on the same page." Now, I am not so sure.

In "the good old days," for the most part, moms did not work away from home. Several years ago, I had an elderly Sunday school teacher who was adamant that a married woman should not work outside the home for any reason. His philosophy on the matter was that if a woman wanted to work, she was expressing a discontent with the provision her husband (and God) was making for her and was, therefore, in the wrong. The idea is not totally without merit, I have to admit.

There is a lot to be said for young children being raised by their mother instead of a daycare worker, who may or may not be qualified or willing to "bring up" your children with your core values, traditions, and expectations; not to mention the confusion and uncertainty that can result from children living under two sets of rules – one at home and one at daycare.

In most families, Mom and Dad are the best choice to raise their own children. Even if a daycare provider shares your core values, the "raising" of the child is not the same, especially in their "formative years." Behavioral and emotional issues that are difficult to "undo" may develop as time goes by.

Because I believed it was very important for me to raise my own children; when my firstborn came along, I opened an in-home business so that I could be home with him all day, every day. When my boys started school, I went to work at the public school they attended, so I could monitor their education and have the same holidays and "home days" they had.

Of course, this is not an option for everyone. But it does demonstrate that solutions may often be found if people sincerely desire to stick to their "family values." Are you compromising your family values today? If so, are you willing to look for ways to remedy that reality, today?

LIFE BEHIND BARS

IN CALIFORNIA

BLUE AND WHITE,

BLACK AND RED,

GOLD AND SILVER,

ORNATELY FABRICATED
BARS ON WINDOWS,
LOCKING
SOME IN
AND SOME OUT :

PRETTY PROTECTION,

SORRY PICTURE.

We have come so far to end up nowhere – in a dark alley that is getting more dangerous and frightening every day. *Or so it seems ...*

Following one of my first trips to the Los Angeles area in the early 1980s, I wrote the poem, *Life Behind Bars*. As I travelled through the seemingly-endless city, virtually every house and apartment had bars on the windows, and I perceived them as a sad-but-true reality for city dwellers. Many of the window bars were ornate and attractive, but the need for them spoke loudly of a reality that was harsh and unattractive.

Coming from a part of the country where we never even had to lock our doors until the last few years, I will freely admit that I know very little about life in the inner city. Less than 1/3 of my first 18 years was spent living inside the city limits of an incorporated town – and it had a population of 603. The largest city I have ever lived or worked in had 50,000 people, and I was there less than three years, more than 30 years ago. I am literally a "small-town" girl with small-town values.

My primary question on this issue is, why do we, as citizens of the greatest country in the world, continue to tolerate the crime that plagues our streets and our neighborhoods? What are we waiting for?

Criminals used to be afraid of light. Many of them are committing crimes, unafraid, in broad daylight today. Many of them are committing crimes, undeterred, taped by video cameras today. People are burglarizing homes in broad daylight with the family at home. People are jacking cars in broad daylight with infants and toddlers in the car and dozens of witnesses. Bold? Not really. Desperate? Undoubtedly. Uncivilized? Absolutely!

There are reportedly inner-city areas in our country where the police will not go because they will surely be killed if they enter. This concept is almost beyond my comprehension. It is time the citizens of America took back their communities and ran out the vermin whose values have eroded to a point where they fear no law, no judgment, and no wrath of a righteous God.

A big bank account and a team of lawyers can get virtually anybody off in this country! Why do we allow our justice system to operate so ineffectively and continue to put us, and our property, all at risk?

Family values will continue to disappear if we do not do something to change this downward slide very soon. This is not something that "somebody else" is going to take care of. WE have to take care of it – and sooner than later.

It has been reported that there are grass-roots efforts here and there across the country, and there has been some demonstrated success; but there has to be a means and a movement to empower more communities and neighborhoods to stand up to gangs and hoodlums and violence in the streets.

Those who are gifted in coming up with solutions to this critical issue need to step forward with their tallest boots on, with their best shovel in hand, and start digging as fast as they can.

In February of 1987, I wrote one of many letters to the editor of our small-town newspaper. For about six weeks, I had been keeping a journal of news stories on corruption and immorality among men who should have been providing a solid example for our children – men we were supposed to be able to trust. Judging from recent news stories, that letter could easily have been written for the here and now. Here is what my letter said.

"To the editor:

A story in <u>The Clarion</u> *(Feb. 16) about the priest molesting the alter boys in Louisiana struck a raw nerve. I had heard about it before, but didn't realize how many were involved. Add to it three out of five Vermont Supreme Court justices accused of sexual misconduct; Iowa Sen. Al Sturgeon facing a paternity suit; and Thomas Coffee, chief investigator in a Mat-Su murder case ordered off the investigation because of alleged sexual relations with a witness before questioning her (all since the first of the year), and you have a recipe for disaster with these being only a fraction of the ingredients.*

My God, if we can't trust our priests, our Supreme Court justices, our senators and our criminal investigators, who can we trust? It's no wonder I see so many young people today with no 'respect for their elders' when these are the examples being set for them. It is a problem which causes me a great deal of concern, just beginning to raise a young family and wondering whose examples my son will have to follow when he is a young man.

I'm not saying there aren't any good young people or there aren't any good examples for them to follow. There are lots of them; but since my graduation from high school 13 years ago, I have observed so great a difference in the attitudes of many of the young people with whom I have been acquainted that it scares me to death. I don't know exactly what we can do about it, but I do know that we can start by making it perfectly clear to the people who are supposed to be examples for our children that we won't tolerate such behavior. If enough people speak up, they have to listen."

Does this sound like a letter to the editor I could have written yesterday? It does to me. I am sorry to say that, if anything, the situation is worse now than it was then.

ONE FLESH

Once upon a time there were just two people (one man and one woman) and God. The people, being mere humans, managed to mess up their relationship with God, with a little help from the devil, himself. There were not two men or two women in the Garden of Eden. If there had been, none of us would be here!

The Bible is not the least bit unclear about intimate relationships outside our gender being unacceptable. It has been suggested that people who condone gay and lesbian behavior should try plugging two male electric cord ends together and see if they can get electricity to flow. They call electric plugs and plug-ins male and female for a reason. THEY CANNOT PERFORM THE FUNCTION THEY WERE CREATED FOR INDEPENDENTLY OF EACH OTHER!

When they marry, a man and a woman are directed to "leave and cleave" and become one flesh. They become two halves of one whole spiritual being. Two men or two women literally cannot become "one flesh." It is anatomically impossible.

Humans were created by God to be different and special so we can "be fruitful and multiply." If we continue on this path of becoming more and more accepting of relationships between people of the same gender, we will eventually reap the results. We are already hardly producing enough babies in this country to sustain our population. The potential consequences of failure in this area are dire, to say the least.

Every time a man and a woman join their bodies, they create "one flesh." This was designed to be a special union that is only entered into following a marriage ceremony between a man and his bride. When an individual becomes "one flesh" with multiple partners, that individual eventually loses such a large part of himself (or herself) that there is no longer anything "special" in any "one flesh" relationship.

Men need to marry women and commit to stay married for life. Men and women need to work together to raise their sons and daughters to be moral men and women. We can find our way off of this sinking ship if we all commit to standing up for what is right and refusing to tolerate or accept what is wrong. Man cannot put asunder ...

If the trend toward not only permitting, but "honoring" relationships between two people of the same gender remains unchecked, it could certainly be the downfall of our society, as, according to the history books, it has been the ruination of other societies in the past.

SODOM AND WHERE?

Do you sometimes wonder if America is on a path to destruction? I don't wonder. It is written all over our society's continuing downward spiral into uncivilized behaviors and lack of respect for each other and ourselves – not to mention God, who will deal with all of this in His own way and time.

It is critical that we stop this erosion of our society into immorality and depravity before it is too late to recover. This issue is getting closer to being too deep to shovel with every day that passes.

Frighteningly enough, two men "partners" can adopt a child in some states. A non-parent former female homosexual partner can get custody of a woman's blood child when the woman turns away from a former "lifestyle" and gets married to a man. Unbelievable, to a "Christian girl" who was not "raised like that." I NEVER thought I would see such events occur in my lifetime. Boy, was I mistaken!

Jesus loved sinners, but he did not tolerate sin. He said, "Go, and sin no more."

THIS MEANS EVERYTHING TO ME ...

In the winter of 2010, I listened to an Olympic athlete describe the four years of intensive training that culminated in a spot on the Olympic medal podium. I had heard the term "medalled" before, but I had not heard the term "podiumed." Believe it or not, there is a new verb called podiumed. I am not even sure how you spell it. I medalled and I podiumed, this means everything to me.

Each time the Olympic games roll around, we hear many stories about the "sacrifices" families make in the quest for athletic fame and fortune. Some Olympic athletes spend literally years of separation from their families to (hopefully) be better at their sport than the next guy or gal.

It is not uncommon for Olympic-prospect children to leave home and live for years in boarding facilities hundreds and sometimes thousands of miles away from their families with virtual strangers for their new "family." People even go so far as to change their national citizenship and the legal spelling of their names to sound more like the names in the country they are competing for. Wow! I had never realized that until 2010.

Being better than someone else in a sport – any sport – should (in my opinion) never be a reason to break up a family for years at a time. An athletic contest being "everything to me" – twisted thinking, to say the least, that excelling in a sport would cause families to make such extreme and potentially emotionally-harmful choices for their children.

Yet another degradation of the traditional family unit – everything ... and nothing. Perhaps I am wrong, but the "glorification" of "star" athletes, from football players to pro golfers and everything in between has gone way too far in our culture. It has, overall, led to an undermining of family values. This convoluted mindset – "this means everything to me" – has created the circumstance in which families are willing to live separate lives – for years at a time – in the interest of competing in a sport. Family values are set aside – to gain what? Fame and fortune ... accolades ... eventually disappointment and loss ... ?

A RECIPE FOR ABUSE

Although I know the problem is not "new," it seems like "child abuse" is more and more prevalent as the years go by. News reporters share horror story after horror story about children who are burned, frostbitten, broken, shaken, and killed. And beyond physical abuse, sexual abuse is rampant.

Are we not as shocked as we used to be by the stories? By the shattered lives? By the utter depravity of it all? One thought on why this may be so much more of an "in-your-face" issue than it was in the past is this:

Mom's third boyfriend this year is not in the least bit invested in her children (none of which are his), so when he is left to baby-sit that fussy, teething six-month old with no parenting skills and no attachment, (maybe throw some drugs and alcohol into the picture) you cannot expect a different outcome than the baby with the shaken-baby syndrome and broken bones who may or may not survive his or her hospital stay. The ingredients for abuse are all there – the result is not ever going to be different until WE do something to change it.

Since there are obviously many young people growing up today without any parenting skills, communities need to come together to help identify and educate individuals who may be at risk for such behaviors. We need to be especially watchful and not allow abuses to go on for years before anything is done.

Mothers and fathers MUST be responsible for care and nurturing of their children and do whatever it takes to ensure that they are in the hands of people who will care for them, not terrorize, injure or kill them. Parenting is a selfless, sacrificial commitment for decades. Those who are not willing to make the commitment should not have children, plain and simple.

Although parents SHOULD be ultimately responsible for raising their own children with moral values and societal boundaries, there is some truth in the statement that "it takes a village to raise a child."

OH, HI JANE; HE'S DOING WHAT? WHERE? THANK YOU SO MUCH FOR LETTING ME KNOW!

In the small town where I grew up, you could always count on somebody's mom calling your mom if they saw you doing something they knew you were not supposed to be doing. My mom received such phone calls from time to time. We raised our children that way, too. They knew, beyond the shadow of a doubt, that any and all of our friends and acquaintances would call us if our children were observed doing things they were not allowed to do. We, too, received such phone calls from time to time.

The key to the success of this child-rearing "tool," I believe, is that all of the parents in our circle of friends and acquaintances share the same core family values. I am not sure that can be said about the average community in America, today.

This concept is also dependent on people not being afraid to "butt in" to your family life. Too many people take an, "It is none of my business," attitude and do not place that call when they see children engaging in inappropriate behaviors.

We are seeing the undeniable results of our failure to participate manifested now.

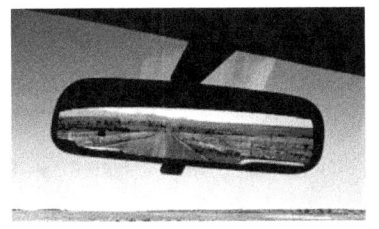

WHERE DID GRANDMA GO?

Once upon a time, Grandma took care of the little ones for a working mom, albeit, the working mom was more likely to be working on a family farm or in a "Mom and Pop" store than in an office in town.

In my part of the country, grandparents sometimes lived in the same house, or at least on the same property. Some of them still do. More families should give it some thought and make it a reality.

Today, Grandma and Grandpa sometimes have to work until they are nearly 70 before they can afford to retire! Grandma, even if she lives close enough to take care of your children, may very well be working just like you are and not be available to care for anyone's children unless she runs a daycare.

LOOKING TO THE FUTURE

- WHAT IS WRONG WITH THIS PICTURE? A LOT! OUR CONTINUED JOURNEY TOWARD ANNIHILATION OF MARRIAGE AND THE FAMILY AS WE KNOW IT WILL ULTIMATELY BRING US TO DESTRUCTION.

- LEGISLATING MORALITY IS OBVIOUSLY NOT THE IDEAL ANSWER, BUT IT MAY BE THE ONLY WAY TO KEEP THE ISSUE IN CHECK LONG ENOUGH TO KEEP OUR HEADS OUT OF THE MIRE UNTIL WE CAN GET THE SHOVELING DONE.

- APATHY IS NOT THE ANSWER! WE NEED TO QUIT BEING AFRAID OF OFFENDING SOMEBODY – ANYBODY – AND TELL IT LIKE IT IS. SIN IS SIN AND WILL HAVE TO BE DEALT WITH EVENTUALLY – EITHER IN THIS LIFE OR THE NEXT.

- MY HUSBAND AND I RENEW OUR VOWS EVERY YEAR ON THE ANNIVERSARY OF OUR MARRIAGE, SO WE ARE NEVER NOT ON OUR HONEYMOON. PLEASE CONSIDER TAKING THIS STEP TO "RENEW THE GLUE" THAT HOLDS YOUR MARRIAGE TOGETHER. A PERPETUAL HONEYMOON IS AWESOME!

MESSY ISSUE #6

OUR CHRISTIAN ROOTS

WORDS ON PAPER IN CLEAR BLACK AND WHITE:

"WE, THE PEOPLE OF THE STATE OF ALABAMA, IN ORDER TO ESTABLISH JUSTICE, INSURE DOMESTIC TRANQUILITY, AND SECURE THE BLESSINGS OF LIBERTY TO OURSELVES AND OUR POSTERITY, INVOKING THE FAVOR AND GUIDANCE OF ALMIGHTY GOD, DO ORDAIN AND ESTABLISH THE FOLLOWING CONSTITUTION AND FORM OF GOVERNMENT FOR THE STATE OF ALABAMA."

Preamble, Alabama State Constitution [7]

Okay, the question is grammatically awkward. But beyond that, how COULD we?

Here is an easy test for you. Where do you think laws that prohibit murder, stealing, breaking contracts, sleeping with your neighbor's wife, etc. originated? Need a clue? God, through the Ten Commandments given to Moses and the Israelites, set forth these laws – our laws. Laws for all generations.

Is there anybody in your circle of friends and acquaintances who does not believe that murder should be against the law? That contracts should not be broken? That thieves should not be arrested and prosecuted? Our value system did not appear out of thin air, America, it was given to us set in stone.

Our core value system has been passed down from generation to generation since Creation. We did not come up with any of it ourselves. What possible justification could our society have for letting our core value system slip not-so-quietly away?

Virginia Bill of Rights June 12, 1776
SEC. 16. That religion, or the duty which we owe to our Creator, and the manner of discharging it, can be directed only by reason and conviction, not by force or violence; and therefore all men are equally entitled to the free exercise of religion, according to the dictates of conscience; and that it is the mutual duty of all to practice

Christian forbearance, love, and charity towards each other.

...duty which we owe to our Creator ... duty of all to practice Christian forbearance, love, and charity ... sounds like Christian <u>roots</u> to me!

Massachusetts Constitution, 1780

Art. II. The governor shall be chosen annually; and no person shall be eligible to this office, unless, at the time of his election, he shall have been an inhabitant of this commonwealth for seven years next preceding; and unless he shall, at the same time, be seized, in his own right, of a freehold, within the commonwealth, of the value of one thousand pounds; and unless he shall declare himself to be of the Christian religion.

The governor "shall declare himself to be of the Christian religion" ... sounds like Christian <u>roots</u> to me! (Even if the wording was later modified.)

Rhode Island Constitution

Section 3. Freedom of religion. -- Whereas Almighty God hath created the mind free ...

Maybe it is just me, but this does not seem to me to be at all unclear. Have there been changes here and there over the ensuing years? Yes. But the "roots" are obvious and consistent.

SEPARATION OF CHURCH AND STATE: NOT!

"A Bible and a newspaper in every house, a good school in every district – all studied and appreciated as they merit – are the principal support of virtue, morality and civil liberty." *Benjamin Franklin, March 1778.*

"It cannot be emphasized too strongly or too often that this great nation was founded, not by religionists, but by Christians, not on religions, but on the Gospel of Jesus Christ. For this very reason peoples of other faiths have been afforded asylum, prosperity, and freedom of worship here." *Patrick Henry*

"Of all the dispositions and habits which lead to political prosperity, religion and morality are indispensable supports." *George Washington*

"Our constitution was made only for a moral and religious people, it is wholly inadequate for the governing of any other." *John Adams, 1798*

"No people ought to feel greater obligations to celebrate the goodness of the Great Disposer of Events and of the Destiny of Nations than the people of the United States. His kind providence originally conducted them to one of the best portions of the dwelling place allotted for the great family of the human race ... Under His fostering care their habits, their sentiments, and their pursuits prepared them for a transition in due time to a state of independence and self-government ... And to the same Divine Author of Every Good and Perfect Gift we are indebted for all those privileges and advantages, religious as well as civil, which are so richly enjoyed in this favored land." *James Madison, 1815*

There are so many quotes of America's founding fathers that I could fill all of the pages of this book with them. However, I will not bother to include more – my point has been made. If you wish to research further, check out the many websites that have compiled noteworthy quotes.

America is a country built on faith in the God of the Bible; and *the further we stray from that faith, the closer we will get to wading into a mire that will be much too deep to ever shovel our way out of.*

INSULATION WITHOUT ISOLATION

Is it possible to have "insulation" without "isolation" in America in the 21st Century?

Throughout my lifetime, I have not ever considered myself an isolationist, but I do wonder whether allowing so many "foreigners" to become a permanent part of our nation today is a truly good idea, especially if they are not required to learn our language and our history. *And even more so because we have millions of American citizens who are currently unemployed who need less, not more competition for the jobs that are, and will become, available.*

I am pleased to see a push to go back to requiring those desiring to become U. S. citizens to meet more stringent requirements. It will make me unpopular in certain circles, but I also believe we must require new citizens to speak, read and write our language – English. This is the 21st Century – anybody can learn English!

The term "melting pot" has never been entirely pleasing to me as a descriptor for American culture. Items melted together over a fire commonly become something completely different than they were before. They lose all individual identity and become a muddled blob of goo. I don't know about you, but I personally do not think I want to be a "gooblob."

Yes, we should be encouraged to retain a love of the "culture" of our native land and people. But there should be no "Little Seoul" or "Little Havana" in America. There should be no "Cuban-Americans" or "African-Americans" or "Korean-Americans." Americans are Americans, PERIOD! *I am not a "German-Welsh-English-American." I am an American.*

As more and more people who are not of the Christian faith permanently come into our country, we will eventually lose our identity as a Christian nation through simple attrition. We are likely closer to that eventuality than most people realize.

Regardless of religious faith, the values of some immigrants, legal or otherwise, are not the values of our founding fathers (and of many of us today). What is important to us is not always important to them. If we get to the point where the majority of Americans do not subscribe to the same value system as we do, where will that leave us? Are we willing to risk that?

Are there new American citizens who are even more excited about being a part of the American dream than many of us are? Absolutely! The diversity of our people is part of what makes America what she is, but we need to work to preserve the common thread of Christian faith and values to hold it all together and to ultimately have God's blessing upon our country and its people.

In this 21st Century world, we really need to think about how many people of any faith, from any nation, we allow into our country each year – for any reason (and that includes college students). The humanitarian in me goes along with the idea of providing asylum to worthy individuals who are under threat of being killed in their own countries. But this privilege must be reserved for a very limited number of those who have no possibility of being a threat to us and who have convincingly demonstrated a willingness to become "real" American patriots.

Some individuals who desire to come here "for a better life" should, perhaps, stay in their own home countries and work toward making changes there, rather than "escaping" to our country.

The first time I ever heard that polling places in America had to provide translators for people to vote, I literally could not believe my ears. How did we get so deep in the mire that we do not require American voters to be able to read a ballot in English? This does not make any sense to me! We are enabling new citizens to refrain, indefinitely – perhaps permanently – from becoming a true part of America – one nation. My America speaks English!

The application for free or reduced-price lunches in America's schools is available in more than 25 languages. Why? What is the paperwork cost for having these documents available? If people want free lunches for their school-aged children, some of them for 13 or 14 years of their lives, then maybe they should learn to read and write English.

This is an issue we need to stand firm on, if for no other reason than the incredible amount of money that has to be spent providing bi-lingual teachers (for 25+ languages in some cities?) and translators for all types of government services. How absurd, really!

While we are on the subject of "foreigners," why are there so many out-of-country adoptions of children allowed every year in this country? Why is anyone in America allowed to adopt a child from any foreign country while there is even one child living in an orphanage – or "permanently" in the foster care system – in our own country? We should take care of our own first.

PATRIOTISM: LIVING FOR GOD AND COUNTRY

[pā′tri-ot n. one who loves his country]

Patriot. What comes to mind when you hear that word? A "loyal" citizen? Loyal to what? The core beliefs of the country where that individual makes his home? Passion? A passion to ensure that the country and its people prosper and are blessed? Sacrifice? Willing to die for what you believe in?

If you polled American youth today and asked them to name five patriotic American songs, how many do you think they could name? If you asked them to recite one line of <u>any</u> American patriotic song (besides *The Star Spangled Banner*), how many do you think could accomplish that task?

How many 21st Century young people cannot even recite one line from *The Star Spangled Banner*? Do you think they know the verse that says, "... Blest with victory and peace, may the heaven-rescued land praise the power that hath made and preserved us a nation! Then conquer we must when our cause it is just, and this be our motto, 'In God is our trust ...' "

Do school children today know who Francis Scott Key was (he was a lawyer) and why, in 1812, he wrote the original poem that became our National Anthem in 1931?

Do we teach our children to be "patriotic" in the 21st Century? Patriotism is not genetic. It is an acquired attribute. Do the little children sing patriotic songs in class in the schools in YOUR town? Do you care? Are you willing to do something about it if they don't?

When they explain to public school children why they do <u>not</u> have to join in the "Pledge of Allegiance," do they also explain why they should WANT to learn it and understand it? Does anyone explain allegiance to one's country? Our ultimate allegiance is to God, Himself; but, we should feel a strong allegiance to our great country, America!

Do you get tears in your eyes when the flags and the marching bands go by in the 4th of July parade? I do. Does it stir something deep in your heart and soul to witness a 21-gun salute at a cemetery on Memorial Day or Veteran's Day? Do you jump to America's defense when you hear criticisms voiced? As many faults as our country has, I do. And there is no reason we cannot be working to make our country better as the years go by.

If we, as the current generation, do not pass a sense of patriotism on to our children and our grand-children, my fear is that the concept of patriotism will die out completely and there will be no "loyalty" to America at all in future generations.

Who are you going to enlist to fight for "nothing"? Who will defend our country in the future if we continue on this path?

We hear more and more about a "global economy" and "global banking" and "global communications." We must be diligent to safeguard our identity as American citizens. We are not "the world," we are America!

Until and unless we bring back the idea of living "for God and country" to the United States of America, we can expect God to not bless this land. Our whole faith must be "pinned on God," and our loyalty must be to "God and country." *Did you notice which comes first?*

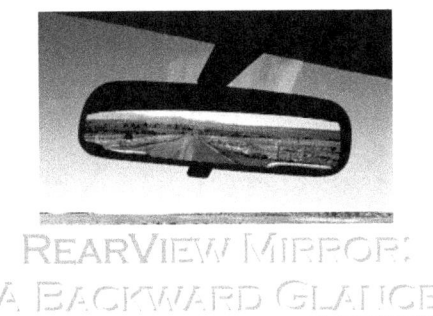

Never, never pin your whole faith on any human being; not if he is the best and wisest in the whole world ... C. S. Lewis

ARE THE HOLES WE'RE TEARING IN THE FABRIC TOO BIG TO MEND?

Sometimes, when I am watching the television news, I wonder if I have gone to sleep and awakened in some other country besides America. Many of the news items seem totally "foreign" to me. It is disheartening to watch our country plunge toward ruin and feel like we are helpless to do anything about it.

All anybody has to do is visit wallbuilders.com to see how closely the standards of the God of the Bible are woven into the fabric of our great country. The evidence is abundant and clear-cut.

How can people be so blind? Is it that they are just not paying attention at all? Are they so absorbed in their day-to-day lives that they are not listening? How did we get so apathetic?

LOOKING TO THE FUTURE

- AMERICA WILL NEVER BE ALL IT CAN BE UNLESS WE RETURN, AS A COUNTRY, TO OUR CHRISTIAN ROOTS.

- THE VERY FABRIC OF OUR NATION IS BEING TORN IN HALF.

- DO YOU REMEMBER HOW TO STOP A RIP? YOU HAVE TO GO BACK BEYOND WHERE THE RIP BEGINS AND MEND IT THERE (KIND OF LIKE A CRACK IN A HORSE'S HOOF).

- WE HAVE TO MEND THE FABRIC NOW, NOT LATER.

- I REMEMBER WHEN PEOPLE WERE SERIOUS ABOUT FINANCIAL RESPONSIBILITY AND WERE TOO "PROUD" TO ACCEPT CHARITY. IS IT POSSIBLE WE NEED TO RESURRECT THAT ATTITUDE AND ETHIC?

- MUCH OF THE ISSUE WITH ILLEGAL IMMIGRATION CAN BE SIMPLY AND READILY SOLVED BY WHAT SEVERAL STATES ARE NOW DOING: MAKE IT ILLEGAL TO RENT TO OR EMPLOY ILLEGALS. *NO PAPERS, NO HOME, NO JOB ... NO REASON TO STAY!*

MESSY ISSUE #7

HEALTH AND HEALTH CARE

IGNORANCE ISN'T BLISS, IT'S BLARNEY!

How did we, as the most highly-educated and "intelligent" people in the 21st Century, end up so ignorant? Americans should be the healthiest people on the planet. The amount of money spent in this country on "health food," "organic food," and "health supplements" is incomprehensible, to put it mildly.

The human body is marvelously and purposely designed to heal and repair itself. In many cases, the two primary factors that are required for this to be successful are proper nutrition and rest. Many Americans do not get adequate quantities of either of those; and *in spite of our high level of knowledge and the availability of everything we need to get and stay healthy, we are overall an unhealthy lot.*

The President and others keep repeating over and over that 47 million Americans do not have access to health care. Maybe ... and that is heavy on the maybe ... 47 million Americans who would like to be covered are not covered by a health insurance policy; but EVERY American (and everybody else who is not an American who lives here) has access to health care. Our little community has both a hospital and a clinic (subsidized by the taxpayers, of course) that offer a sliding scale to individuals and families who are of limited financial means.

QUIT saying that many Americans do not have health care. Many Americans do not have health insurance. Then again, many Americans do not WANT health insurance. They never mention that group when they are talking about either health care or health insurance.

The first year I worked for the school district where I am still employed part time, I was making about $600 per month. My health insurance premium was $300 per month. I went to the doctor once in 12 months to have a "female checkup." So, I paid $3550 of my $7200 wages for a $50 checkup. Makes perfect sense to me! Not!

The next year I cancelled the health insurance and put the $3600 in the bank. That was nine years ago. I have been to the doctor exactly twice in the ensuing years, for a "female checkup" both times.

Under the contract negotiated by the union that I do not belong to, at present, the State of Washington contributes well over $400 per month for my medical insurance policy, with a $750 deductible. How it could cost that much to insure one healthy person, (dental and vision are separate) I cannot fathom.

And now, the President and Congress would like to tax that contribution from the State of Washington as part of my INCOME. I did not ask for them to contribute it. Why should I have to pay income tax on it? I have received no benefit, whatsoever from it, during any of the past five or more calendar years. It has been at least five years since I walked into my doctor's office. The cost of the policy for nine years is nearly $50,000, for one person, with ZERO output to doctors, pharmacies, or any medical facility.

School district employees, at least in my "neck of the woods," are highly educated, physically fit, almost never smokers, and one of the largest "people pools" in the country. So why does it cost so much for insurance for school staff? What would the premiums for insurance be if this was NOT one of the largest pools of workers in the country?

I grew up in a family that was uninsured. It never kept any member of the family from seeing a doctor or going to the hospital when necessary. You simply made sure you had money in savings (or made payments in the case of something catastrophic). My parents did not expect someone else to pay for their health care. Neither did they go to the doctor (or take us kids) for every little sniffle.

DELINEATING THE "FAULT LINE"

There is no doubt that some of the fault lies with American insurance companies. Many products and services are willingly overpaid by insurance companies – and WE allow it (by doing nothing about it). It is really fundamentally no different than auto insurance, where there is no doubt whatsoever that there is a difference between what "people" pay and what "insurance" pays for the exact same products and services. Auto repair companies will tell you so point blank, and I have experienced it first hand.

We all know that insurance companies have to have a lot of money in reserve to pay out claims. But their executives do not have to make millions in salaries and bonuses while the VFW holds spaghetti-dinner fund raisers for the local cancer patient's family! We have gone beyond reason into something I cannot even name – why do we put up with it?

In the mid 1970s, a young married couple in our family delivered a premature baby that cost probably three and a half years' worth of their family earnings. They lost their home and had to go back to renting – and they made payments to the doctors and hospital until their daughter was probably 10 years old. BUT, they did not expect to be "bailed out." They ultimately recovered from the financial setback, raised their family, and currently own and operate their own business. The "baby" is now a mother, herself.

For those of us who come from healthy lineage, practice healthy lifestyles, and only have to see a doctor every two or three years for a less than $100 checkup, paying several hundred dollars per month for insurance seems totally ludicrous. Those who insist that insurance is needed "just in case" are not looking at the issue from the same viewpoint as I am.

Another part of this issue is our need to "fix everything" – "play God," if you will. I grew up with people who were "crippled" or "indisposed." People accepted them as they were. Family members often cared for them. It was commonly a demonstration of sacrificial love. Are we going to legislate away sacrificial love? Not every illness and injury requires professional care.

Somehow, we have to find a balance between fixing what truly needs fixing and leaving some things alone. It is my personal opinion that no "cosmetic" surgery should be covered by insurance unless it is for someone burned in a fire, a crime victim, or someone injured in some kind of tragic accident. Elective cosmetic surgery should never be covered by insurance. It costs us all money in escalating insurance premiums.

I have not seen the numbers on how many surgeries are performed in the U.S. every day, or how many body parts are replaced. It would probably knock me over to know. Perhaps I am better off not knowing. Personally, I do not want to replace my body parts. A new body in Heaven is what I am looking forward to!

Too many of the people in my circle of friends and relatives who have experienced surgeries or hospital stays in recent years have come home – or ultimately ended up – in worse condition than when they went in. Several of them picked up infections that literally almost killed them. One of them died. Several had procedures that were done incorrectly or "artificial parts" (like a hip joint) were recalled and had to be removed and replaced, requiring anesthesia, surgery, and recovery AGAIN – for what? Because somebody, either in the hospital or the manufacturing facility, did not do their "job" correctly. So who can we trust with our health?

Stories like this make me not want to ever go to a hospital! There are more than a few instances every year where healthy people go into a hospital for a "routine" procedure and come out in a body bag. The frightening reality is that checking into a hospital could kill me. Doesn't sound like "health <u>care</u>" to me!

WHY ARE WE KILLING OURSELVES?

Why do Americans not help each other to be more healthy? How many times do we sit idly by while our friends, neighbors, and relatives literally ruin their health before our very eyes? Do we speak up? Do we make loving suggestions? Do we care whether they kill themselves or not?

How can we remain so ignorant in the midst of the "information age"? Everyone who can read has access to virtually unlimited health and wellness information, including question-and-answer forums on legitimate medical websites online. If you do not have internet access, virtually every American has access to a free public library and/or a book exchange.

Do I believe everything I read? Of course not. When something sounds reasonable, I check for multiple, authentic sources that agree and weigh the information based on facts and a healthy dose of common sense.

Hazard a guess on the answer to this question. How many foot, leg, hip, back and neck problems are created by people wearing improperly fitting shoes, high-heeled shoes, or untied shoes? Answer: a lot!

Common sense tells me that sloughing along with your shoes untied is bad for you. Do you know how many teens I see walking with their shoes not properly tied – or not tied at all – today? Is it any wonder they eventually develop problems with their hips, legs, feet and backs? Shoes were designed to fasten in a particular way so they fit properly. So, tie your shoes!

When I was in my early twenties, information came out that wearing high-heeled shoes was really bad for women – bad for their backs, their legs, their feet. The information came from a reliable source and it made sense, so guess what? I quit wearing high-heeled shoes. Guess what else? Thirty years later, I do not have the back, leg and foot problems many of my women friends who wear high-heeled shoes have.

In 21st Century America, many people never walk into a shoe store that has employees on staff to determine whether the shoes you like and want actually fit your feet. Discount shoe stores are pretty much "self-serve," and shoes are too often selected that really do not fit properly at all. It's a health issue.

Here is another question: When we know so much about the toxic properties of many hair dyes, lipsticks, nail polishes, shampoos, and other cosmetics, why do we continue to use them? Patches were created for modern drug and therapeutic applications because we absorb things through our skin very efficiently. What are you absorbing into your body tissues and bloodstream every day? Do you know?

We advise people to get more exercise, then send them out to walk and jog alongside streets and highways to deeply breathe into their lungs some of the worst air in America and pound their bones and joints to ruin. We advise people to drink more water and they buy cases of plastic bottles filled with water that comes from who-knows-where and does who-knows-what to our sophisticated body systems.

We tell people sitting in a recliner is bad for their backs, then we sell them a reclining loveseat and add more channels to the cable or satellite TV package.

Is the chlorinated water people bathe in, swim in, drink, and cook with knocking off the healthy bacteria on and in our bodies and upsetting our digestive and other body systems? Is it contributing to the emergence of superbugs? I found out years ago that using anti-bacterial soaps would logically contribute to the emergence of superbugs and quit buying it. There is such a thing as "too clean."

How many people know that not chewing your food long enough creates a failure to produce the necessary chemicals so that your body can process and digest food correctly? They used to teach children how many times to chew their food. How many people understand that many gastric issues are from a shortage of "stomach acid," not an excess of it? How many people eating antacids by the bottle are making their problem worse, not better? Does it seem reasonable that drinking too much water before or during a meal might dilute gastric juices so they cannot work properly? Do you care whether your food is properly digested? Does nutrition matter to you?

Ten years ago, tired of wasting gas and membership fees to go to the gym to exercise, my family bought a "home-gym" for under $200. It still works great. More than 20 years ago, I bought a compact, folding cross-country ski machine at a yard sale for $25. It still works great and is one of the quickest, best whole-body exercise methods that exists, in my opinion. Is your fitness worth $25-200?

Who do you know that could not do a few stretches each day to preserve flexibility of the shoulders, neck, spine, hips and legs? How many surgeries are performed and medications are used each year in America for issues with the shoulders, neck, spine, hips and legs? Stretching does not take very much time, and it does not cost ANY money.

REFINE THIS ... PRESERVE THAT

When and why did we start eating white bread and refined sugar? Why do we accept having a list of 35 ingredients on a tub of guacamole or a cracker box? The first time I actually stopped and read the ingredients on the guacamole carton, I started making my own guacamole. Preservatives are the #1 reason. We want food items to have a long shelf-life so they are always available. Well, maybe what we "want" is making us sick and we need to make some changes in the way we process and store food.

Why aren't we eating better? In many places in our country, it IS difficult to get quality, locally-grown fruits and vegetables for a reasonable price; but I would guess that in some areas, they are more available than you might think. Have you checked?

Many cities now offer garden co-ops and buying clubs. There is no doubt that if people would eat more whole foods, more "real" foods, they would be ultimately healthier. Maybe more cities should take a look at unused buildings that could be torn down to make space for "mini farms." Can you say co-op?

It is possible for people on a restricted budget to eat well. Our family does it all the time with careful shopping and making a lot of our own foods. Fortunately, my family lives where we can grow and can/freeze/dehydrate some of our fruit and vegetables, as well. I do understand that not everybody in America has that option. But we all have many options and choices for our health and wellness.

Why should those of us who eat healthy foods and take good care of ourselves be punished, in a sense, for our responsible actions? This messy issue is really about choices, and our inability to make good ones – isn't it? *It does not make sense to me why people would choose to be unhealthy.*

HEALTH IN THE GARBAGE CAN!

It was announced this year that First Lady, Michelle Obama, was embarking on a "crusade" to fight obesity in American children. I hope she succeeds. One of the ideas was the "been there done that" issue of making school lunches more healthy. People have been trying to "healthy up" school lunches for at least 20 years, if not longer.

Besides being too costly to really consider (on the huge scale of feeding the children in every school in America multiple meals each day), much of the "healthy" food served to school children today goes directly into the trash can, which is a real American tragedy.

I first encountered the issue of fresh fruits and vegetables dumped, untouched, by students in the trash can (and unopened cartons of milk and juice) in the mid 1990s when I worked in an elementary school lunch program. We were serving red, seedless grapes, kiwi, cantaloupe, bananas and all sorts of wonderful, incredibly expensive, fresh fruits and vegetables to our K-6 school children – items many of us could not easily afford to buy in the store for our own families in rural Alaska. I was totally blown away by the <u>unbelievable</u> amount of this fresh food that ended up in the trash can on the way out of the cafeteria. And it is not that different in many schools across America today. Many, many children do not LIKE and will not eat costly fresh fruit and vegetables.

Should we try to get our school children to eat nutritious foods? Of course. Should we pay literally tens of millions of dollars annually nationwide for that healthy, expensive food to be thrown in the trash – two meals a day in many schools? *I find it hard to justify continuing to put that burden on taxpayers,* many of whom cannot afford the same food at home.

In our elementary-school breakfast program, which was used by many students from well-to-do families whose moms just did not want to get up in the morning to feed them breakfast, I witnessed child after child take a disposable tray with a breakfast burrito or other breakfast main item on it with fresh fruit or juice, and milk. At least 60% of them went straight to the trash can and threw everything but the juice or milk in the trash without even looking at it.

Growing up in a small, conservative community whose attitude was "waste not, want not," I never imagined people were capable of doing such a thing! How can we be so wasteful, America?

And beyond that, an unopened carton of milk could not be saved to give to a six-year old who had forgotten his lunch money. It had to be thrown away because milk (and the meal) was federally subsidized and it would interfere with the "count."

Surely, funding this wanton wastefulness cannot be cheaper than an occasional "theft of goods" by the rare someone who over-orders for their own benefit. The waste <u>has</u> to cost us all more! Besides, it is just plain wrong to waste that much usable food. Isn't it?

However much money is being spent, and however much food is being eaten or thrown away, the bottom line is this: Are there legitimate, accurate statistics showing any benefit from school breakfast and lunch programs? Are the children better educated? Are they healthier overall than school-aged children 40 or 50 years ago? I doubt it. The obesity statistics among children today are pretty conclusive. Does that denote failure of the school meal programs?

Unless we can figure out a way to provide cost-effective, nutritious school meals that the majority of children will actually <u>consume</u>, this is going to be an ongoing problem, even with the First Lady's help.

In addition, many high school students in an open-campus situation prefer to go to the drive-through or the deli to get their lunch, rather than eating what the school provides, so providing a nutritious lunch on campus does not benefit that group of students in any way (nutritionally).

It is entirely possible that regular exercise is even more important for school children than school meals, in terms of battling the obesity issue.

TAKING CARE OF #1

Earlier this year, I caught my toes on the corner of the blanket chest at the end of my hall – a nauseatingly painful experience – and probably broke at least one of the bones in my foot.

As I do with every "trauma" injury, I immediately took the first of what would be several doses of arnica (a homeopathic remedy). Because I do not believe in seeing a doctor unless it is obviously <u>necessary</u>, I dug through the bathroom cupboard and came up with:

1. An ankle brace one of the boys had used for football,
2. a piece of foam from a forearm stabilizer,
3. two elastic bandages,
4. a piece of cardboard

Using my fully capable brain, I fashioned these items into a protective stabilizer kind of like you see people walking around in after they have gone to the doctor with a foot injury.

When asked by co-workers if I had seen a doctor, I pointed to my "stabilizer" and replied, "He would have just put me in one of these." And everyone who inquired about the injury agreed that was true.

The first couple of days, I could not bear any weight at all on the foot and I used yard-sale crutches to get around. After eight days, my foot began to heal itself and I went to just the elastic bandage in a roomy, open-toed shoe. Another ten days later, it was still tender, but functioning normally.

Add some zinc and extra vitamin C to help the body do what it was designed to do – heal itself. A little massage, a few sessions with a yard-sale "foot bath" and some Epsom® salts – good as new! Today, the foot is fine. The cost of "treatment"? Under $5.

We have so many resources available today in terms of books and online "MD"s, it is not that hard to take care of ourselves. We just have to DO it. You can even shop at yard sales or used book stores for informational and recipe books like the American Heart Association and the American Diabetes

Association publish. Verify information with multiple, reliable sources that agree.

Most of us are capable of taking care of ourselves most of the time; and we should choose to do it more often. Read, study, learn. Use your judgment for when to see a doctor – and take care of #1 whenever it is not obviously risky for you to do so.

Keep in mind that if my foot had not been appreciably better in 10 days, I would have seen my family doctor, with or without insurance. The key is determining when to see a doctor and when to "do it yourself." We are smarter than we give ourselves credit for. Yes, we are!

WHY DOES "HEALTH CARE" COST SO MUCH?

It is a true statement that Americans do not have access to "affordable" health care. Being subsidized by the government or paid for by insurance does not make expensive health care cost any less. The expensive health care just costs the taxpayers or those who pay insurance premiums a lot of money instead of the patient. (Kind of like an individual paying $80 per month for a "low-income" apartment that the government is paying $720 to subsidize. The people who own the apartment still get $800 per month.) Health care costs far too much in 21st Century America. The "payee" is irrelevant.

MACHINES AND REPLACEMENT PARTS

Testing, testing, one, two, three, five, ten – too many tests is one reason health care costs so much. There is big money in testing – really big money. It has been reported that people may be getting cancer from improperly high levels of radiation in some of these widely-used testing machines. Being diagnosed with cancer from a test you did not even need in the first place would be very hard to take.

We all know that the top-of-the-line, leading-edge new machines and technology used in medicine today have a great deal to do with the cost of medical care. The cost of some of the 21st Century's medical "miracle machines" is almost "out of this world!"

My husband's suggested solution to this is: if the government really feels "it" should be involved in health care, then have them buy the machinery for the hospitals and medical facilities so they do not have to recoup that expense in their cost of providing services.

The per-day cost of a hospital stay, anywhere in the country, is ridiculously high. Twenty-first Century hospitals are huge facilities with huge operations, maintenance and personnel budgets – and they have to meet their expenses somehow! We all know how.

REPLACEMENT PARTS

Replacement parts, whether they be a mechanical heart valve, a transplanted kidney or an artificial shoulder joint, cost a fortune. People who make $18,000 per year cannot ever hope to save enough money to pay for an organ transplant surgery or an artificial joint.

MALPRACTICE INSURANCE

Thanks to ambulance-chasing lawyers and America's "sue, sue, sue" attitude, malpractice insurance is a huge factor in the cost of practicing medicine today for both hospitals and individual care providers. My doctor in Alaska used an arbitration agreement in lieu of an expensive malpractice insurance policy, which was perfectly fine with me.

Yes, there should be compensation if a doctor or medical facility makes a known error and a life is dramatically changed (or even ended) needlessly. Some settlements are so totally beyond reasonable, though, that this must be limited in some way. Are there too many lawyers in the legislature to enact tort reform? The outrageousness of the few costs the many much.

MEGA-BILLING

There is little doubt that the union wages in every phase of health care are a contributing factor to today's high costs. I have never understood how those of us who make $8-15 per hour can be expected to pay $45-300 per hour for "professional" services. This is seriously out of balance, especially when what we are discussing is, for the most part, a matter of critical need, not luxury or vanity.

Why does it cost $920 for a non-gold tooth crown? Who can afford that? Deep cleaning an entire mouth costs more than $1,000 – a <u>month's wages</u> for some of us. How can they justify that? It is partly because that is what insurance will pay. *If there was not an insurance policy forking over the dough, they might not be charging that much.*

By the way, how much sugar is in your toothpaste and your mouthwash? You don't suppose the toothpaste manufacturers have stock in the dental industry, do you? I am not fully convinced that all of the deep cleanings and "extreme maintenance" are not causing some people to have more problems than they would have had without the "maintenance."

Why does a set of quality hearing aides cost $6,000? Sure, it is a mini-computer; but I can buy a computer for $500 or less. An iPod™ is a mini-computer. But it does not cost $6,000. My mom could use a good set of hearing aides, but she could never afford to pay $6,000. Even $1,000 seems to me a ridiculous price for hearing aides. They are a quality-of-life necessity, not a vanity purchase. Nobody buys hearing aides unless they truly need them.

As long as 20 years ago, I had a relative who experienced some serious health issues and was hospitalized multiple times. The total bill over a several-year period was more than half a million dollars. HALF A MILLION DOLLARS! And that was 20 years ago. The 20%, over and above the 80% paid out on her behalf, equalled around $100,000. This was a retired couple on a very fixed income. Fortunately, they had inherited some money. Otherwise, they could never have paid out that much money.

Regardless of whether people have or do not have insurance, the cost of "health care" is ridiculously high and it should not be so. This is human beings' lives we are talking about. What a world we live in, where some people can financially afford to "live" and some cannot.

The total kicker is, after all of my relative's tests and hospital stays, they never did figure out what was wrong with her. Half a million dollars into the "health care," she died not knowing what was causing her underlying health issue. "Practicing" medicine …

That part of this messy issue is not about health insurance at all – it is about the outrageous cost of a stay in the hospital and of medical procedures, themselves. It is about sue-happy lawyers and their sue-happy clients. It is about the difference between what we need and what we want. Medical care does not have to be so expensive. We allow it to be.

THE "PLOT" TO PUT EVERY AMERICAN ON AT LEAST ONE PHARMACEUTICAL PRODUCT

"Nothing is more fatal to health than an overcare of it."
Benjamin Franklin

Turn the television on any time of day or night and you will find a seemingly unending string of commercials for pharmaceutical products – and there are more new ones all the time! Some days I will see advertisements for two new ones in the same day. More ... and more ... and more ...

My "theory" is that there is a plan by somebody, somewhere to have every American on at least one (and probably more than one) pharmaceutical product, for something that is perceived to be "wrong" with them, within the next few years.

Add government health care to that and you have a guaranteed, no-boundaries income for pharmaceutical companies FOREVER! Now, there is a frightening thought for American taxpayers!

It may or may not be true, but years ago, I heard that the pharmaceutical companies could not market a product unless it had been approved for at least one disease or disorder. People, can you not see how many diseases and disorders have been "discovered" in recent years? Can I prove it is an organized "plot"? Of course not. But, it sure makes a lot of sense to me that there is something behind the idea. How many more new "disorders" are we going to be suffering from and treating with pharmaceuticals in the coming decades? Someone should keep count.

Pharmaceutical advertising encourages people to focus on all of the things that could possibly be "wrong" with them. I have "restless leg syndrome" – you know, the one where you feel like you have to get up and move.

Guess what? That is what I do. _I get up and move_ – I stretch and massage the muscles in my lower back, legs, feet and neck (yes, restless legs can start in the NECK). And guess what else? The "get up and move" feeling goes away within minutes! Who'd'a thunk ... it doesn't take an MD to figure that one out.

The muscles in the backs of your legs tighten up as you sit, especially if you have been sitting a long time. A simple stretch of the lower back and legs, accompanied by deep breathing, before you get up can make a huge difference in how not only your legs, but your lower back and pelvic area feel when you stand up and start to walk after an extended period of sitting – especially if you are "older," like me.

Please note that I agree there might be people who are not helped by stretching, massage and homeopathic remedies. It makes me wonder, though, if their doctor suggested stretching and massage as a precursor to pursuing a pharmaceutical solution.

Based on what I have learned, I am pretty sure that if anyone had heard of A.D.D. when I was a child, I would have had it. Actually, I am pretty sure I still have it. Undiagnosed and untreated, it did not keep me from graduating in the top 10% of my class, though!

Observe how rapidly the frames change on the television screen today. How can that NOT be effecting how young children develop language and reason? It makes me nauseated to watch it, sometimes, and I have to look away. There is no way a child can process images and language that rapidly. Or learn language from cartoon or animated characters whose mouths do not move like the human mouth moves in speaking words. Children learn from watching mouths move, not just from hearing words. Get them out from in front of the TV, especially when they are very young, and see if less of them "need' pharmaceuticals to cope with processing language and reason.

All you have to do is read and listen to the long and frightening list of possible side effects to be convinced that the risks of taking many pharmaceuticals do not equal, much less exceed, any possible benefits to your "health." People end up taking additional measures to combat side effects – and it creates a domino effect for some. Do you know how many times DEATH is mentioned in the "possible side effects"? "...to do no harm ..."

Many people in our 21st Century world are ultimately NOT more healthy or enjoying more "quality of life" as a result of the pharmaceutical products they are using.

Several times each year, stories emerge about pharmaceuticals that are being questioned, or even pulled from the market, because the research has finally caught up with the reality that they are doing more harm than good. We really are the "test rats" – AFTER the products are approved for sale. Lucky us!

Are there good, helpful, life-saving pharmaceuticals? Yes! Does everybody in America need to be on one of them? No!

Why do drugs need to be advertised on television at all? Your doctor should know what is available and make recommendations to you. You don't see ads for chemotherapy drugs, do you? Or blood-pressure medicine? They don't advertise "water pills."

They only advertise products for "discretionary" health issues, it seems. "Ask your doctor if this might be what you need," they suggest. "Ask your doctor; and be sure to tell him if you are taking this, this, or this ..."

In addition, I am more and more convinced that the furor over cholesterol levels is a pharmaceutical marketing tool. Count heads in your immediate circle of friends and family members and see how many of them are on a "cholesterol-lowering" drug. How many of them are healthier overall since they have been taking the drug(s)? How many of them have made diet and exercise changes for their overall health – or are they relying on pharmaceuticals to take care of the "problem"? How many of them could just eat more food fiber and naturally lower their cholesterol?

How many drug advertisements say, "along with a healthy diet and exercise plan," in the fine print at the bottom of the ad? Do people try the healthy diet and exercise plan first, and then add the drugs if that fails? Do their doctors advise non-pharmaceutical options before prescribing drugs? Is it just "more convenient" to take a pill than actually DO something about nutrition and healthier living?

Why is this a "messy issue"? Because millions of Americans are taking pharmaceuticals they may not need. Many people are more sickly on them than off of them. And many of the drugs are paid for by either insurance companies or the taxpayers. Which means YOU are paying for them. And if you cannot afford them, the generous and compassionate pharmaceutical companies advertise that they may be able to help you get your drugs – their drugs.

There is no end in sight to the stream of new drug ads that will pop up on our TV screens with someone who seems "just like us" trying to convince us we should talk to our doctor about one or more of them. I just saw a new one today. It looks like it might be one that is being introduced to replace another one that was recalled because it was unsafe.

This is a messy issue because we are being taken advantage of, often to the detriment of our overall health, and we should not allow it! Why do we continue to allow it? This is an area where we have the ability to take control, and we fail to do so.

WHY DO WE CRY "FOUL" WHEN OIL COMPANIES POST RECORD PROFITS, BUT NOBODY SEEMS TO NOTICE THAT PHARMACEUTICAL COMPANIES ARE RAKING IN TOP U.S. INDUSTRY PROFITS WHILE FEEDING ON PEOPLE'S FEARS AND PHOBIAS?

How much pharmaceutical companies are profiting off the fears and phobias of the human race is in the news from time to time, however, it is seldom "reported" in a negative light. After all, they are "helping people," aren't they? With your money!

There are literally dozens of pharmaceuticals for "depression." What happened to learning to cope with life? How many pharmaceutical products assist people in skirting around coping with "life," or avoiding it (coping) altogether? How can that be healthier for people in the long run? How is that different or better than escaping life with alcohol?

America, we need to really put some time and thought into assessing our genuine need for pharmaceutical products, as well as mandate that the FDA and the pharmaceutical companies KNOW something is safe before they turn it loose on the American public. We must stop being satisfied with "acceptable" side effects and find solutions with NONE.

It seems logical to me that these companies believe they need to pump such a high percentage of their budgets into marketing and advertising because people really do not "need" a lot of the products they offer. We can trust our doctors to prescribe what is best for us. Can't we?

There is too much money in this industry, and too many outrageous executive salaries and benefits, to trust pharmaceutical companies either to police themselves or to have an honest desire to REALLY make our lives better for the long term.

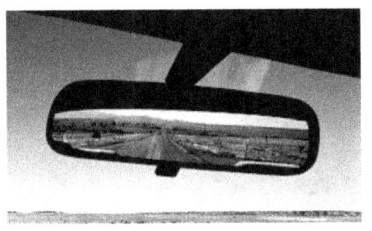

AN OPEN INVITATION!

Insurance companies and pharmaceutical companies are in business to make money. They have shareholders who want to see steady earnings in their quarterly reports and their bank accounts. Because their end "consumer" is a person in need of medical assistance, however, medical insurance companies should not necessarily be treated the same way as any other for-profit free-enterprise "company." Reaping profit from people who are sick or dying is dancing on a fine line between "good" and "not-so-good."

The idea that a business or medical facility (be it medical, auto, or homeowners related) can charge a certain amount just because that is what an insurance company will PAY for that service is preposterous and an insult to the American people. This is simply an open invitation for greed and corruption. It is a guarantee that costs will escalate and insurance premiums will increase accordingly.

Looking to the Future

- There needs to be real reform, not only in health insurance, but in all other forms of insurance in this country, as well.

- As long as we keep paying up, health care providers will keep charging whatever they want.

- If we are required to purchase insurance, we have lost all of our bargaining power as consumers! This happened with auto insurance, and it will happen with health insurance.

- There will probably never be a realistic solution to cases like the one in our news in July of 2010 about the man who was electrocuted and incurred hundreds of thousands of dollars of hospitalization costs he could not (and did not) pay, after he allegedly tried to steal electric wire from atop an electric pole in a live electric transmission line. Care was provided and somebody had to pay. Pretty simple ... Wow!

- People need to go back to taking personal responsibility for their own health and making informed choices for nutrition, exercise, and wellness.

- We really need to find out for ourselves whether foods and "medicines" are bad for us and not just blindly follow the advice of the "experts," who do not have that great a track record, when you get right down to it.

MESSY ISSUE #8

EDUCATION

21ST CENTURY EDUCATION'S
INSTITUTION OF THE 4TH R

Bond issue after bond issue fails, classrooms fill up and coffers are depleted.

Union contracts bind a declining school district budget and dictate the shifting (or lack of it) of employees to make the best use (or not) of those who remain after the pink slips go out.

It is a huge "catch 22" that has no clear remedy. Bankrupt school districts, mothballed buildings, shorter weeks and longer days. Educating 21st Century America should not be such a financial struggle, folks. So what is our problem?

WHAT'S NOT SOCIALISTIC ABOUT TODAY'S EDUCATION FUNDING?

If you don't think we are already socialized in America, just take a close look at education funding. The federal government has taken over funding in so many areas, and the control over how the money is spent lies entirely with upper-level government agencies. If a local district does not spend the money as directed, they lose it. The federal government has no business in funding education. It is not making education better.

In an effort to attempt (heavy on the attempt) to make sure every American child gets an equal education opportunity, complicated formulas have been created to calculate education funding.

Local school districts have little say in how they can spend their education dollars for the benefit of the most children in their particular district. America, we need to tell the feds "NO" and return to trusting our local school districts to do their jobs.

There is no way that what is good for an inner-city school district in Chicago is the same as what is good for our rural school district where there are still some folks who do not have electricity in their homes.

Oh, I know. It is all about making sure that no American student gets "left behind." America, we need to dig our way out of the "left behind" pit. Unfortunately, this will never be achieved by approaching the problem from a "national level."

THE TRAVESTY OF SPECIALIZED FUNDS

Your science department needs new textbooks. Your special education account is overflowing. Your vocational account is overflowing. But you cannot take money from either program to buy science textbooks. So you continue using the textbooks from 1974. What is wrong with this picture? Everything!

We must return control of school funding to the local level so that each district can make judgment choices on where education funding will be best spent for their students and their community. This is not an "option" folks, this is a "must" for American children.

The "apron strings" for federal education funding need to be cut, and it needs to be done now! Can you chop an apron string in two with a shovel? You can with the right "chopping block" behind it!

IS LITTLE JOHNNIE READY FOR COLLAGE?

No, it is not a typographical error. C-o-l-l-a-g-e is how far too many high school seniors spell college today. Dumbfounded, I will ask you this: how do you get to 12th grade without learning to spell college?

Back in the early 1990s, when my boys were in grade school, our district brought in a couple of new programs that were supposed to help our students learn to both read and write more proficiently. One of them encouraged teachers to stop correcting spelling because if a child had to stop and think about whether he had spelled a word correctly, it would interrupt his flow of thoughts and, therefore, inhibit his writing.

The theory was that students would "pick up" the ability to spell as they went along through their years of school. Let me tell you, folks, new is not always better. We have probably millions of school children in this country who never learned how to spell properly before they graduated from high school. And this is not only allowed, it is encouraged in districts all across the country.

Part of the problem with education today lies with standardized testing and the way districts end up spending money so their students can (hopefully) score well on mandatory standardized testing. There have been questions raised about the validity and necessity of standardized tests for decades. I remember one example that was given at a state-wide conference I attended in the early 1990s.

As I recall, the test included a "question" that portrayed a picture of an ironing board and a garment on the board, with an iron and a human arm and hand also in the picture. The correct answer was the verb "iron."

Many, many elementary-aged students across the country did not come up with the correct answer to that question. No surprise. Many of the adults attending the conference where I saw the example did not come up with the correct answer, either! Still no surprise.

While watching a *Jeopardy* episode in mid 2010, I was shocked to watch as none of the three incredibly-intelligent adult contestants could identify a color photo of an Appaloosa horse. As someone who has owned Appaloosa horses, I had an "edge" over three people who have education far above mine.

This is exactly the point that was being made in the presentation with the "iron." People in different areas of our country learn different things. Their lives are different. Their homes are different. Their cities and towns are different. Their jobs are different. There is <u>nothing</u> "standard" about our huge and diverse American landscape and population.

Maybe if we just had all students in America's schools watch *Jeopardy* and *Are You Smarter Than a 5th Grader* for 12 or 13 years, we would end up with "educated" children. Even Ivy League college graduates cannot answer many of the questions on either show, but their deficiency in proficiency is obviously not due to lack of "education."

With the money we spend on pre-K through 12 education in America, we should turn out the brainiest brainiacs on the planet. So why don't we?

BUDGET CUTS DUE TO ENROLLMENT

Budget cuts due to declining enrollment hurt in a number of ways. A district's fixed costs do not change much unless they actually close buildings or sell them.

Whether you have 300 students in a building or 500, you still have to keep the rooms at a certain temperature. The lights still have to be on. The computers and copy machine are still running in the office. The district office still has to manage what buildings and programs remain open. Federally-funded programs require very specific staffing, training and record-keeping to administer them.

The only real "flexible" area in most school budgets is staffing, which is generally 80-90% of the budget, so districts end up combining schools, sharing staff between buildings, and packing more students into each classroom when district enrollment (and the per-student finding that goes with it) declines.

THE UNION FACTOR: UNIONS AND TAX DOLLARS ARE NOT COMPATIBLE "PARTNERS"

Everyone who knows me well knows that I do not believe <u>any</u> taxpayer-funded entity should be subject to a union contract. Not firefighters, not policemen, not garbage collectors, not educators.

When a non-union, for-profit company has to tighten its belt because of changes in the economy or markets, choices are made to cut everything from multiple locations to across-the-board wage and benefit cuts for all employees, so they can at least attempt to all stay employed. They work together to do what is best for the company AND the most employees.

Whether it is the underlying intent or not, the fact is that union labor contracts create a wall between labor and management. Union contracts create "them" and "us," not "we"; and loyalty to your company or organization is sometimes completely lost in the mix. This is <u>not</u> the work ethic I grew up with.

When an entity funded by declining tax dollars is bound to one or more union contracts, the taxpayers are held "hostage," by people who may be dissatisfied making far more in wages and benefits than YOU are (or ever will be) making. Huge decreases in income, sales, excise, and property tax revenue collected during our current economic crisis have demonstrated this concept again and again across the country.

Many years ago there was a garbage collector strike in a major city and the whole country watched on the television news as the garbage piled up day after day on the streets. The heaping mounds of refuse eventually created a critical and dangerous health hazard for the citizens of the city and made me question where the "public" fit into the term "public servant." An "agreement" was finally reached.

A labor strike is a muted form of blackmail. There is no other way to define it. That is why strikes occur. Threat is a powerful motivator for prompt settlement of the issues being "negotiated." If it was not so, they would not bother to strike (or threaten to do so).

When teachers strike, it always effects students and parents, in addition to the teachers and other staff members (including bus drivers). When schools close because of strikes, working families are forced to scramble to arrange child care or stay home with their children (sometimes without pay).

This pushes the "wave" into the business realm, where businesses are left dealing with employee absenteeism or extra costs to pay two people – the one staying home on personal leave and the one replacing him or her.

Every day such a strike continues is a day the school will have to make up at the end of the year, sometimes well into the summer. In a large district, literally thousands of families may have to cancel vacation plans and change work schedules. Schools with no air conditioning create a health hazard for students, staff and the teachers who, by their strike, caused the school year to extend into hot summer months. Threats of strike bring fairly rapid settlement to contract negotiations because nobody in the administration or on the local school board wants to be held responsible for creating such havoc. There has to be a better solution.

Many local unions insist on members "working to the rule," which nixes volunteerism entirely. Staff members are not permitted to "go the extra mile," themselves, but still have to carefully explain to their students how volunteerism is a mandatory requirement in their senior portfolio.

Please do not misunderstand. There are many, many school employees who DO come before and after school and "volunteer" their time and effort to ensure student success in their districts all across the country. God bless every one of them!

But there are districts in America where teachers and classified staff volunteering their time is not only discouraged, but is forbidden by their unions.

READING, 'RITING, 'RITHMETIC, 'RECTIONS ... 'RECTIONS?!?

Reality check! Last time I had the opportunity, if you want to call it that, to listen to a presentation given to public high school freshman on "sexually transmitted diseases" by representatives of the local health and social services department, my face must have been bright red for half an hour afterward!

In my almost 55 years of life, I never imagined that we would be "teaching" our young men and women (in a mixed-gender setting, no less) such explicit material (I cannot even relate their teaching material in this book; it would be considered pornographic!) or that "we the people" would be encouraging our 14- and 15-year old young men and YOUNG LADIES to practice putting a condom on a banana so when they need to use one (implying that they WOULD need to use one), they could do so correctly and rapidly to hopefully stave off sexually-transmitted diseases and/or unplanned pregnancy.

People, we cannot continue to turn a blind eye to this "teaching" of filth to our young people in our public schools! It has got to stop.

Yes, parents are generally allowed to "opt out" their children; but given my experience, it is unlikely that parents fully understand the reality of the shocking, graphic material and explicit information that is being shared with the students in some of these situations. Unless the parent goes to the school building at the appointed time and place to check, there is no guarantee that the student did NOT attend the presentation against the wishes of the parents.

This very messy issue made the news in more than one area of the country in the summer of 2010, as some districts have proposed discussing sexual issues with children as young as age five, including using the correct, anatomical names of body parts.

"They" say somebody has to teach America's children about "reality" and their parents are not doing so. "They" say that the children are having sex whether or not any of us approve, and we have to "protect" them somehow. What a messy issue this one is! Never in my wildest dreams did I imagine that American education would come to this. Never!

"TANSTAAFL"

"There ain't no such thing as a free lunch."
Uses of the phrase dating back to the 1930s and 1940s have been found, but the phrase's first appearance is unknown. [8]

In the mid 1970s, I spent some time as one of the "Symms Girls," (the other members of the group were girls I had met at Girl's State). Our "job" was to drive around in a truck with sideboards on it, promoting Steve Symms for congress. Congressman Symms used the acronym TANSTAAFL in his campaign. (I think it was the first time I actually ever knew what an acronym was.)

I have always believed that the idea was sound. No matter who is "giving" you something, someone is paying for it. I touched on this idea briefly in the chapter on politics, taxation and government.

Education in America is no different. Our children receive a "free' education in public schools in this country; but are we really giving them an education worth having? Are their lives remarkably better for having been through America's "free" public education system? With the escalating cost of public education, American taxpayers certainly do not feel like the education is "free."

In some classrooms in some schools, the time spent on student learning in a day is minimal. There are a number of factors that play into this tragedy, including "crowd control," traveling back and forth to the library to use computers, dozens (and sometimes hundreds) of students absent multiple days per week to attend athletic or other extra-curricular events, and substitute teachers in far too many classrooms on far too many days of the school year.

So, we could assert that, "There ain't no such thing as a free public education." If you ask me, our public education "free lunch" is leaving a bad taste in our mouths.

How About We Educate Our Own College Students First?

While we are on the subject of education, we might as well talk a bit about college. I am getting pretty tired of reading stories about students from foreign countries who come to America to study at virtually no cost to them. Free housing, free books, free tuition (free medical care).

We have plenty of our own young people who deserve a post-secondary education and cannot afford it because our colleges and universities are expending all of their "freebies" on students from countries besides our own.

It only makes sense that if the colleges and universities were not spending so much of their resources on educating foreign students, they would be more financially able to offer all American young men and women a less expensive education. It does not take an accounting major to figure that one out.

We are forcing many of our young adults to graduate from college with $100,000 or more in debt, supposedly justified by the "need" to have that education to get a decent job, while we educate foreign students for pennies.

One of our three sons currently in college completed his FAFSA last year and reported that the government's calculation of his "family obligation" was $400 (toward non-resident tuition at the University of Arizona's Eller College). The "aid" that was offered to him, however, consisted of a small grant and an offer for private loans at 12.5% interest. Some aid!

How about we take care of our own for the next 30 years and see how it goes? If there is money left over at that time in the college endowment funds and the U. S. government treasury, then we can talk about giving foreign students what we seem to be unwilling to give our own!

"MAINSTREAM" IS "OLDSCHOOL"

I do not give a lot of credence to discussions regarding the relationship of what American students know – or do not know – compared to children of other industrialized nations. We are talking about "apples and oranges" on that issue.

Many of the discipline problems encountered in schools in America today, both public and private, can be traced to the decline and dysfunction of the family unit. Our schools cannot take up all the slack in people's failure to properly raise their children at home.

Many of the "other" problems in schools in America today are issues that trickle down from districts being forced to commit too many resources to underlying discipline problems and too many resources (and dollars) to preparation for standardized testing. Most of the problems in our schools today could be solved without any additional tax dollars being spent.

Looking to the Future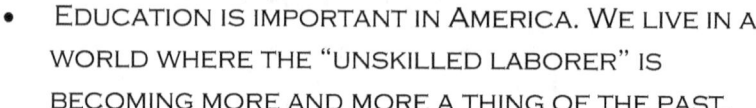

- Education is important in America. We live in a world where the "unskilled laborer" is becoming more and more a thing of the past.

- We cannot dress everybody in a suit and place them in an office cubicle, however. SOMEBODY has to learn carpentry, masonry, and machinery operation. If they don't, who is going to build your next house?

- When I was in grade school and in high school, the teacher put those of us who were ahead in the back of the room (or another room) tutoring those who were behind. We should consider doing more of that again. They call that "peer tutoring" today. We did not call it by any name back then.

- Because students learn at different levels and by different means and methods, we absolutely should encourage charter schools, gender-separated schools, and content-focused schools so that every American student has the opportunity to make the most of his or her educational opportunities.

- We will not know if "new and improved" types of schooling will work unless we try them on a broad enough scale and for a long enough time to make a reasonable assessment of their value and success (or lack of it).

A FINAL WORD

DETERMINED TO MAKE A DIFFERENCE

DEAR TOO-DEEP READER:

It is my fervent hope that by the time you reach this page you will have become determined to take some sort of action to correct (or at least seriously question) one or more of the messy issues discussed in this brief commentary – to make a difference!

Although there are obviously many other issues I could have covered, I included the ones I believe are the most critical to be dealt with by Americans in the immediate future. Perhaps there will have to be a second book to cover the other issues that concern me.

We Americans are resilient folks! If this book does nothing more than spark your interest in doing even one thing to make America a better place for all of us and for future generations, then I have succeeded in my goal.

As frustrated as we may be – or as much as we may feel that our vote does not count – we must continue to participate in the democratic process so that we may be confident we have done everything in our power to effect change in America, for ourselves and for future generations.

Please take a lot of time to research candidates up for election (or re-election) and encourage your friends, relatives, co-workers and acquaintances to do so, as well. We are at a critical time in American politics, and the elections in the next decade will have a huge impact on our country and our citizens – *on whether we have a bright future to look forward to or drown in the hogwash because we allowed it to get too deep to shovel!*

P.S. Power to the polls!

REFERENCES

[1] "influence." *Dictionary.com Unabridged*. Random House, Inc. 12 Feb. 2010. Dictionary.com http://dictionary.reference.com/browse/influence.

[2] "influence." Thorndike, E. L., <u>Thorndike Century Beginning Dictionary</u>, Scott, Foresman and Company, Copyright, 1945 by E. L. Thorndike, p.323

[3] "influence." Black, Henry Campbell, M.A., <u>Black's Law Dictionary</u>, Fifth Edition, West Publishing Co., St. Paul Minn. 1979, p.701

[4] "legislation." *Dictionary.com Unabridged*. Random House, Inc. 12 Feb. 2010. Dictionary.com http://dictionary.reference.com/browse/legislation.

[5] Alter, Bonnie. *Greenpeace to Build New State-of-the-Art Rainbow Warrior III.* http://www.treehugger.com/files/2010/01/greenpeace-new-ship.php

[6] Roach, John. Hydrothermal Vents Found in Arctic Ocean; National Geographic News; January 23, 2003; http://news.nationalgeographic.com/news/2003/01/0123_030123_hotspring.html

[7] http://www.legislature.state.al.us/codeofalabama/constitution/1901/ca-245529.htm

[8] Safire, William. *On Language; Words Left Out in the Cold;" New York Times, 2-14-1993*

Gretchen Slinker Jones was raised and educated in the farm country of Southwest Idaho and continues to study writing. She moved to the "Inland Northwest" in the late 1990s, settling on the fringe of the beautiful Selkirk mountain range, after spending 17 years in Alaska. The owner of a small desktop publishing and business writing firm, Jones specializes in résumé writing for clients all over the globe. Her freelance writing projects included a weekly newspaper column for five years.

The author of *Selkirk Mountain Inspiration and Selkirk Mountain Inspiration 2*, *Your Resume : A "Crash Course"*, and *Your Resume : A "Crash Course" 2*, Jones writes poetry for adults and children, as well as children's short stories. Her poems, currently available as *Song of the Heart: The Complete Collection*, have appeared in numerous anthologies, newspapers and magazines and have won multiple awards. She wrote *Breastfeeding: A Mother's Guide* in 1984 and revised it in 1989 and 2009. *It was re-released in 2010 under the title Breastfeeding Your Baby: The Right Choice*

Selkirk Mountain Inspiration 3 is scheduled for release in November of 2011.

Danny Jones, who contributed to this text, is the husband every Christian woman hopes and prays for.

Author and husband photo taken atop "The Cross Rock" on their property in NE Washington State by J. Shane Morgan

185

For a complete list of titles by this author, visit
www.wordcopro.com

Jesus is coming again!